# FROSTLINES

# FROSTLINES

A JOURNEY THROUGH
ENTANGLED LIVES
AND LANDSCAPES IN A
WARMING ARCTIC

## NEIL SHEA

ecco

*An Imprint of* HarperCollinsPublishers

HarperCollins books may be purchased for educational, business, or sales promotional use. For information, please email the Special Markets Department at SPsales@harpercollins.com.

hc.com

Ecco® and HarperCollins® are trademarks of HarperCollins Publishers.

FIRST EDITION

*Designed by Alison Bloomer*

Library of Congress Cataloging-in-Publication Data has been applied for.

ISBN 978-0-06-313857-5

25 26 27 28 29 LBC 5 4 3 2 1

*For Taylor*

Even a wounded world is feeding us.
Even a wounded world holds us, giving us
moments of wonder and joy. I choose joy
over despair. Not because I have my head in
the sand, but because joy is what the earth
gives me daily and I must return the gift.
—ROBIN WALL KIMMERER, *BRAIDING SWEETGRASS*


Everything is alive in its own way.
—REMY LEE SHEA

# CONTENTS

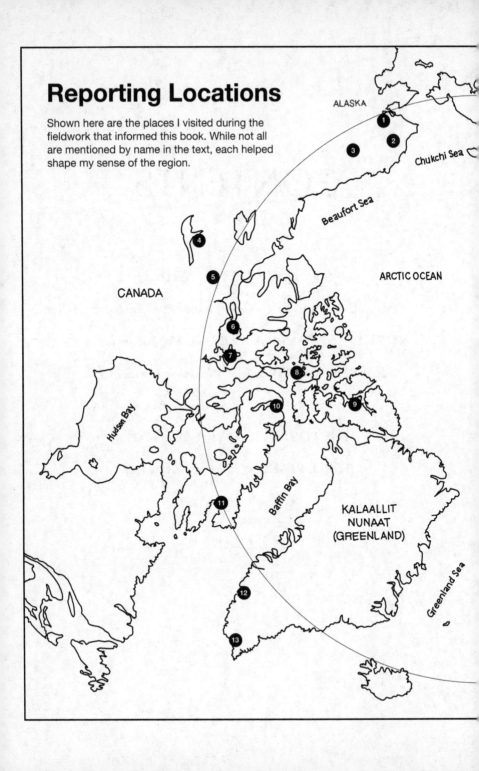

# Reporting Locations

Shown here are the places I visited during the fieldwork that informed this book. While not all are mentioned by name in the text, each helped shape my sense of the region.

ALASKA

Chukchi Sea

Beaufort Sea

ARCTIC OCEAN

CANADA

Hudson Bay

Baffin Bay

KALAALLIT NUNAAT (GREENLAND)

Greenland Sea

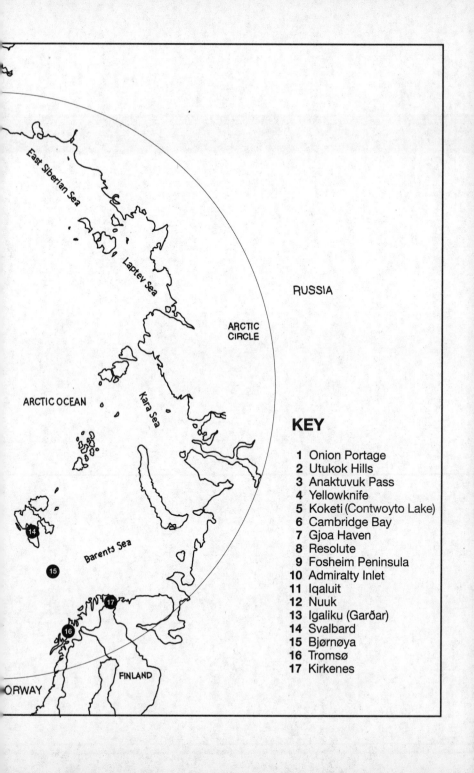

RUSSIA

ARCTIC
CIRCLE

East Siberian Sea

Laptev Sea

ARCTIC OCEAN

Kara Sea

**KEY**

1 Onion Portage
2 Utukok Hills
3 Anaktuvuk Pass
4 Yellowknife
5 Koketi (Contwoyto Lake)
6 Cambridge Bay
7 Gjoa Haven
8 Resolute
9 Fosheim Peninsula
10 Admiralty Inlet
11 Iqaluit
12 Nuuk
13 Igaliku (Garðar)
14 Svalbard
15 Bjørnøya
16 Tromsø
17 Kirkenes

Barents Sea

FINLAND

NORWAY

# FROSTLINES

*Introduction*

# A GIFT OF WHALES

ON A BRIGHT JUNE MORNING IN 2005, I STOOD at the edge of the sea ice in Canada's Admiralty Inlet watching narwhals talk with each other.

Here and there on the dark open water, whales in pairs and small groups thrust their heads above the surface and, very gently, brought their long tusks together. One animal would then slide its tusk along another's, or several whales would gently collide, tusks held aloft in a kind of slippery Musketeer salute.

Over and over for hours the whales convened this way, breaking the sea's glassy surface, hanging there for several breaths, then slipping below in a slough of bubbles. At times the water seemed pierced with tusks, our air world nothing more than a pincushion.

It was my first visit to the Arctic, and I had never seen anything like this. The whales were probably all males (only very rarely do females grow tusks), and it's been suggested that the display is one way males size each other up: literally a biggest tusk contest. There was even a word for the behavior—biologists call it *tusking*.

Tusking? It sounded ridiculous, a kind of linguistic laziness. Like calling speech *mouthing*. Turning the noun into a verb seemed to suggest violence, too, like stabbing or jousting, when the whales' gestures were in fact careful and slow. I observed no obvious plays for dominance. None of the rough spectacle you might expect from big socially ambitious mammals.

Instead, the males caressed each other.

In their restraint, it seemed clear that something powerful was passing between them, and for this we had no language.

TWENTY YEARS AGO, NARWHAL TUSKS WERE MYSTERIous objects, still closer, perhaps, to the unicorn horns they'd been mistaken for in the courts of medieval Europe. The tusks are elongated teeth that spiral out of a male's upper jaw, and now we know they are laced with nerve endings, perhaps making them sensitive to pressure, temperature, and other sensory data in ways similar to human fingertips. No wonder, then, that the whales I witnessed weren't clobbering each other. In recent years, the whales have also been observed stunning fish with their tusks, and apparently playing with fish, too. Other research has shown that layers of the tusk can be read almost like tree rings, offering a view into an individual's diet, say, or its exposure to mercury.

In 2005, none of this was known. It was extremely difficult to study narwhals, for they avoided boats and humans, often diving under the ice whenever researchers tried to draw near. They were among the largest living enigmas on earth.

At the time I was a young staff writer for *National Geographic* magazine, sent north to Admiralty Inlet, on my first big assignment. I was to visit the floe edge, the place where melting sea ice meets open water. In Inuktitut, the language of the Inuit, this place can be called *sinaaq*. My editors had asked me to investigate, to the extent that I could, whether or not climate warming was having any effect on wildlife along the floe edge, but back then climate change wasn't the emergency—the daily alarm—that we know now. Mostly I was there to be a witness, and to bring back a description of everything I saw.

The narwhals, *tuugaaliit*, had only recently arrived, pushing through leads in the ice from their winter grounds in Baffin Bay and Davis Strait, a journey of several hundred miles. With the males were pregnant females, who would soon give birth, and juveniles of previous breeding years. From my campsite on the sea ice, it was impossible to know how many narwhals had reached the inlet, but more seemed to arrive each day, joined by pods of ghost-white belugas and even a few enormous bowheads, which loomed like submarines in the still black water. I was overwhelmed by their numbers, and the whales were merely part of the larger show, which included polar bears, seals, cod, and copepods, along with innumerable birds roosting along the cliffs in the distance.

This gathering at the *sinaaq* was one of the Arctic's most spectacular events and I was a novice, out of my depth in every way. The floe edge vibrated with sex, death, and

feasting under the endless light of the midnight sun. The
scale of the journeys undertaken by the whales and bears
and birds, the icescapes and sea roads they had crossed—
the sheer weight of all those lives converging, colliding—
here were stories that could never fit into any magazine.

For a while I tried anyway. I slept little during those
sun-washed days. I attended to the animals' comings and
goings. Scribbled notes as if the number of words might
somehow match the volume of life. Finally, after many
hours of watching and counting, I surrendered, stuffed
numb fingers into pockets, and just listened to the whales'
wet breath roll over the water. I tried to imagine what they
were saying.

ALMOST A DECADE AGO, A GEOGRAPHER NAMED
Michael Sfraga told me there was no such thing as the
Arctic.

Sfraga, who would go on to become the first U.S. am-
bassador to the Arctic, liked to sketch out what he meant
with numbers: Four million people living in the region.
Some four-hundred thousand of them Indigenous. Dozens
of languages, dozens of tribes and nations and homelands,
all of them scattered across just eight modern states . . . you
get the idea.

"So when you say, 'the Arctic,'" he said, "Which one
do you mean?"

The question gave me a place to begin.

The word Arctic comes from the ancient Greek *ark-
tikos*, which can mean *northern* and is related to the bear

constellations Ursa Major and Ursa Minor. It's a term that's been cast like a net over the northern part of the globe. At its peak is the North Pole, and the ring at the bottom is the Arctic Circle, which runs around the earth at sixty-six degrees north latitude. This net is, generally speaking, why so many people (myself included) have thought of the region in catchall terms: big, cold, white, and far away.

Indigenous perspectives are quite different. In the many dialects of Iñupiaq and Inuktitut, related language families that reach across the North American Arctic from Greenland through Canada to Alaska, the things that make up the far north—land, water, ice, and territory— have many names, though the largest meaning is perhaps captured in the concept of *nuna*. This root word appears in various forms throughout Arctic North America. The word carries a meaning of *land*, but it can expand to describe a sense of country, belonging, or even the territories of animals. You see it in the name of the only Indigenous-governed territory on the continent: *Nuna*vut. It's there in the name Greenlanders call their country (the one that, as I write, U.S. President Donald Trump is aggressively seeking to annex): Kalaallit *Nunaat*. The name of a small tribe I visit in this book, who live only in a single isolated village in the heart of Alaska's Brooks Range, is *Nuna*miut.

I'll use the word *Arctic* going forward for simplicity, but most of my observations, revelations, and travels— most of this book—unfolded in Indigenous *nuna*.

This book is a journey through that space, through many Arctics. When I began to imagine it, the line I hoped to follow went around the top of the world like a thread

pulled through rich fabric and I thought it would be possible for me to travel from Alaska to the far east of Siberia.
That didn't happen. The world changed during the course
of my research and fieldwork. Some portions of the north—
most notably Russia—became impossible for me to enter,
though I could still walk up to the door and peer in. Other
places I dreamed of going were too far away, or too expensive, for me to reach. My own life also changed. When I
began seriously considering this project, my partner and I
had one son. Since then we've had two more. It isn't easy
to leave them, and they are still too young to come north
with me.

The places I have decided to include in this book, while
not linear, do progress through distinct themes. The book
begins in the world of animals and then moves to one of
people. The middle two chapters concern the mingled
destinies of both—humans and animals in relationship.
The final two chapters turn toward ancient disasters and
modern wars and explore how far people will go to survive
when their lives grow more chaotic or they face the end of
their world.

Taken together, the chapters offer a journey through
thresholds—places where, if you look in one direction, the
old cold world can still be glimpsed, in the migrations of
caribou, the hunting skill of an Inuit elder, the discoveries
of young archaeologists gathering clues to unsolved mys-
teries. And if you turn the other way, you'll see the next
Arctic, the *emergent* one, gathering in the near distance.
This is the north that melts, greens, and grows warmer.

This is the space where, to borrow again from Sfraga, "a whole new ocean is opening up before us, and that hasn't happened before." This is the future where nations like Russia and Norway sink more oil wells into the Arctic seabed and where animals no longer keep their old appointments with people.

THE ARCTIC I SAW IN 2005 NO LONGER EXISTS.

Innumerable changes have unfolded since I stood on the sea ice in Admiralty Inlet. Most of them have to do with heat, human-caused climate warming, and the fact that today the Arctic is warming three or four times more rapidly than any other region of the planet. This book assumes you know some of the story.

The heat I'm speaking of is destroying the Arctic cryosphere, that portion of the north that consists of frozen water: glaciers, sea ice, snow, and permafrost. This heat disrupts weather patterns, the migrations of animals, the movements of ocean currents. This heat is disrupting the distribution of plants and animals and people, forcing some out of places they have known for centuries even as others come north into new areas that were once too cold. Heat lets more ships travel through the Arctic and more tourists visit. It will allow more gas, oil, minerals, and fish to be extracted from within and below the Arctic Ocean. This heat is ours, this book assumes you agree, and to this end I won't spend much time diving deeply into the science of climate warming.

Instead, I have tried to tie the stories here together with a sense of the stakes, as the Inuk activist and Nobel Peace Prize nominee Sheila Watt-Cloutier describes them in her book, *The Right to Be Cold*. "What is happening today in the Arctic is the future of the rest of the world," she wrote. "In one lifetime, we Inuit have seen our physical world transform, the very ground beneath our feet shift dramatically." The far north has been mostly left out of southern thinking, she says, condensed across generations into a world of inertia and frigid emptiness.

But a necessary reframing of this dim old view puts cold at the very center of attention, not only in the north but for southerners, too. In the Arctic, Watt-Cloutier tells us, cold is freedom. It's freedom to travel over the ice where there are no roads, freedom to hunt and visit distant kin. Cold is also an invitation to seek and cherish warmth, to create community, to let your life be shaped by weather and animals. Above all, it is cold that binds the many Arctics together, and this in turn has enabled the climatic stability we at lower latitudes have long enjoyed. In the chapters ahead I carry her haunting question everywhere: What can it mean, for all of us, if the north ceases to be cold?

By the time I reached the floe edge on Admiralty Inlet, great upheaval was already well underway. The effects of warming were still not well known and they could be difficult to see. Scientists were talking about it, of course, and many were shouting warnings. But most of the rest of us weren't listening.

In Arctic Canada (and everywhere else in the far north), traditional ways of life had been changing, too, for decades.

By the 1970s, the last of the nomadic Inuit had been lured or coerced into settlements and virtually no one lived on the land anymore. No one used igloos. Hardly anyone kept dog teams or traveled by dogsled because the practice had been discouraged, sometimes violently, by missionaries and government officials.

To get places, Inuit now rode snowmobiles and all-terrain vehicles. They drove boats and cars, climbed aboard jet liners. They came home to watch satellite television and defrost slabs of seal meat in the microwave. All this is to say that the Arctic has never existed outside our modern, entangled world. It is not timeless or inert. I didn't know much about these changes when I went north for my first trip twenty years ago. Since then, I've traveled to the Arctic many more times. Often I've gone as a journalist, working for *National Geographic*, but sometimes I've headed north on my own. And now I see transformation everywhere.

In Admiralty Inlet, one consequence of the warming world seems to be an increase in the number of killer whales entering the region. In colder times sea ice prevented the big predators from traveling in certain parts of the north. Killer whales don't seem to like ice, and one reason may be that their tall dorsal fins do not make for easy or comfortable under-ice travel. This, for the narwhal, offered an enormous protection.

The narwhal is smaller, slower, and far less aggressive than the whale the Inuit call *aarluk*. Killer whales are well-known hunters of narwhals. But narwhals have no dorsal fin, and they are at home under ice. For hundreds or perhaps thousands of years, they have been able to seek refuge beneath it.

In our era, this protective barrier is rapidly diminishing. Almost every summer it seems a new record is set for sea ice lows. The shrinking ice seems to have allowed killer whales into areas they rarely visited or had never been seen in before, including Hudson Bay. Inuit in many places have reported the whales attacking and eating narwhals. There is, apparently, even a specific term for the way narwhals and other species react: *aarlungyuk*, which can mean a fear of *aarluk*. Scientists in Canada have estimated that killer whales may eat hundreds of narwhals per year in their newly expanding range.

Of course the *aarluit* (plural of *aarluk*) can't be blamed for doing what they do. They're merely moving into an emergent world, one humans have helped to create. Like us, they are fast, adaptable, hungry. In a way they have become our avatars. It doesn't do the animal justice to take this analogy too far. But here, in the expansion of *aarluit*, we see the unintended consequences of our appetites.

WHEN I FIRST ARRIVED IN THE ARCTIC, I WAS LESS than a year into my job at *National Geographic*. What I wanted most was to prove that I could handle the work. The assignment was a kind of test, and I was given to know that if I messed up it would be a long time before I was sent anywhere else. So I stayed awake more than I slept, watching the sea with Paul Nicklen, the photographer I was working with, and Andrew Taqtu, a hunter and pho-

tographer from the town of Arctic Bay who had taken us
out onto the ice.

Slowly, the lid of clouds that had hung around for
days pulled back to reveal an endless blue. At that time
of year, the sun never really sets, and somewhere north of
us, in Lancaster Sound, the ice was breaking up, opening
corridors for animals. Each day more arrived. The black-
and-gray-flecked narwhals, often joined by ghost-white
belugas. Countless birds arced through the air—fulmars,
terns, kittiwakes, gulls—filling space with their wingbeats
and chatter. Below them, on the ice, ringed and bearded
seals lay by their *aglus*, their breathing holes.

Polar bears wandered near our camp, too, their fur
sometimes streaked with blood from recent meals. And
once, in a wide channel between shelves of ice, an enormous bowhead appeared. It lay at the surface, calm and
still, so close that I imagined reaching out to touch the gray
scars running over its gleaming black back.

There was little else to do but wait and watch. I carried
a shotgun with me to the toilet, in case of bears. Sometimes,
in the endless evenings, we ate boiled seal with ketchup. In
all of this we longed for narwhals. Whenever we heard their
breath out on the water, we dropped bowls and mugs, shoved
on boots, and ran to the edge. Sometimes they went shy and
disappeared. Other times they began tusking. I remember
asking Andrew what the behavior meant, and he told me he
did not know. All he could say was that the whales seemed
to do it only here, and only at this time of year.

Thinking now of the scale of those journeys—of the
geography and memory represented by the animals' arrival

in that place—is still overwhelming. Some of the seabirds and possibly the whales had crossed the globe. Many of the whales were probably older than I was. Other creatures had traveled hundreds of miles, all of them risking their lives with purpose. And each species had been visiting that spot for generations, perhaps thousands of years. In southern life we don't value patterns and rituals so ancient. We have few equivalent traditions and little regard for such continuity.

I remember the sky and water alive with bodies. In tusking narwhals, in the explosive breath of the bowhead and the expectant hunger of polar bears, you could see acknowledged some kind of inheritance. And, a day's journey away, in Andrew's town, Inuit hunters were tuning snowmobiles, cleaning rifles, planing down the runners of their sleds. They were preparing to join the great gathering, as their ancestors had done, and take a place at the enormous table.

NOTHING EVER CAME OF THAT ARCTIC TRIP.

After a couple of weeks on the sea ice, I traveled back to the States and the story was killed, the first casualty of my career in magazines. I was angry, but also relieved. I wasn't ready to say what I had seen. A year passed, then two, and more. No one ever asked me to write about the floe edge, no one asked me to explain or account for it.

One way I have come to think of that journey is through an old story of the Iñupiat in Alaska. They once believed, and perhaps still do, that whales spend most of their lives dwelling in a country of their own, far beyond the human realm. From there they observe us, judge us, and descend into our world to give themselves to righteous and humble hunters. In this telling, the whales know what they are doing when they allow themselves to be killed. They understand the gift they are giving with their bodies and know their sacrifice will bring great joy to the hunters and their communities. Back then I was no hunter, the whales had not come for me. And yet their gift was so large anyone could've received it.

For twenty years I have thought almost daily of that gift. This book is my attempt to finally meet it and offer something in return.

ON ONE OF MY LAST DAYS ON THE ICE, I BORROWED a kayak from Paul Nicklen and paddled out onto the sea. The water was calm, no animals in sight. The narwhals had vanished. I cannot recall how long they'd been gone, but we worried they would not return to our tiny sector of the vast floe edge. Without them we were bored, irritable, strangely lonely. Paul in particular was stressed—he needed more images, he needed to find a way to get closer to the whales. I paddled out onto calm water under bright sun, but soon the darkness and depth of the sea filled me with a kind of dread. I had never kayaked in water so cold, so deep. After a while I let the boat drift, turned my face to the sun, and thought of drowned explorers.

Then I heard it: the wet-soft breath of a narwhal.

Suddenly I found myself surrounded by a small pod.

They swam close, within feet. I could see their tails, their tusks, watch the light play over their mottled skin. They were curious, investigating, carving wide circles. Males and females rose and dove beside me in the black water.

I whipped around in the cockpit, wondering if anyone else had noticed. Back on the ice, Paul had set up his big camera. He was waving, saying something. Later he told me he was shouting, "Get out of the way!" But I couldn't hear him.

In that moment I thought he was simply as happy as I was. Waving for the joy of it, for the wonder of that place. Awash in the thrill of the narwhals' nearness.

I raised my hands and shouted, "They're everywhere!"

# AMONG WOLVES

*Umingmak Nuna / Ellesmere Island*

I AM STANDING ON A HILLSIDE IN THE HIGH ARCTIC with four white wolf pups. We're staring at one another, wondering how it has come down to this. They're only a few months old and I have been here on the tundra for even less time, so taken together we are all too new to know anything. We are lost at the top of the world.

It's mid-September, about twenty-five degrees Fahrenheit. The sky is pale, colorless, headed toward twilight. Below us Ellesmere Island opens like a map we cannot read. Martian-red soil in the drainages, moon-blue mountains at the horizon. Accordion hills unfolding treeless and bare to the east.

The pups look at one another, then at me, several rounds of nervous glances. *Somebody please do something.* Then, they have an idea. A revelation. It seems to hit all at once. They sit on a bench of bare stone and howl. They howl like the lost children they are. It's a magnificent crescendo, the four voices high and mournful and tumbling down the rocks. You'd think they were a choir, this a hymn, but it's a cry for help.

Somewhere out there is the rest of the pack, five older wolves who walked off an hour or two ago and left me alone with the pups. They're hunting musk oxen. We don't know where they headed, and by now they could be miles away. The pups seem to grasp this and already they know that anything might happen out there on the tundra. This is why I hear a note of panic in their howls. Maybe they've never been left on their own before. Surely they've never been left with a human.

I watch them fill their lungs. The pups aren't very big— each one's a couple of pillows pushed together. They have large paws, though. Carpet-tack teeth. One day, if they survive, they will grow to be seventy or eighty pounds and capable of pulling down musk oxen many times larger. Now, they are hungry as well as lost, and this adds an edge to our misadventure.

My eyes go to the runt, the smallest of them. She is always first to start howling and she holds on longest, as though she understands the tenuousness of her place in the pack. Her breath dissolves into the air. Her eyes are more thickly lined in black than those of her siblings'. After each chorus she resets herself, placing her paws and squaring her shoulders—howling being a whole-body experience—then she turns her tiny ears to listen for an answer. None comes. The pups howl again and listen again. There is nothing but cold and wind and the enormous Arctic silence.

Then, from afar comes a faint cry. They all hear it. Ears

swivel, butts begin to bounce on the rock. The pups howl once more and this time there is a clear and closer answer.

After a few minutes the older wolves bound up the hill. The pack reunites and there is such effusive happiness—whining, face-licking, nuzzling—that the impression is almost one of surprise. It's as though the wolves did not believe they'd see each other again. Maybe the pups really did feel that way, maybe it's just the nature of love in this hard place. A couple of the adults seem to glance at me in reprimand and I shrug to show it wasn't my fault, but the mood is high and there's work to do and soon the family is moving, down into open ground, heading east or was it north toward plains busy with oxen.

I follow behind, as happy as they are and still stunned to have been left alone with wolf pups. I notice the cold now, probing along the seams of my clothing. For a moment it strikes me as strange that cold should make all this possible—the wolves, the oxen, my time with the pups. But up here cold is key. It's the glue that binds this world together and keeps everything else at bay.

I'D LANDED ON THE FOSHEIM PENINSULA IN LATE AUGUST outside a small Canadian weather station called Eureka. The station sits at about eighty degrees north latitude, and it is one of only three inhabited places on Ellesmere Island. The others are Alert, another weather station at the northern tip of the island, and Grise Fiord, an Inuit village along the south coast. Ellesmere itself is the northernmost island in Canada, and at nearly seventy-five thousand square miles it's slightly smaller than Great Britain. Between the weather stations and the village about two hundred people live in all that space. Much of the rest is polar desert: arid, frigid, bare. But this makes it a good place for wolves. Possibly it's the best place of all.

The wolves I had come to see belonged to an unusual population that seems limited to the Fosheim and possibly areas around it. They were known to be remarkably tolerant of humans, and scientists had been able to observe them up close, with astounding intimacy. The wolves' behavior, which is often described as fearlessness, had even allowed researchers to overturn some long-held and less-than-generous assumptions about their kind. The animals' lack of fear had, too, given rise to a handful of documentary films, magazine articles, and photo books, which to my mind tended to cast the wolves as some kind of semi-mystical creature, a species that *looked* familiar, but that in fact we had never encountered before. The truth, of course, is that our kinds have known each other since the beginning.

The Arctic wolf is a subspecies of the gray wolf, *Canis lupus*, which means it's essentially the same animal you may see in Yellowstone National Park, or in the forests of Alaska, or in the mountains of Spain, Italy, China, Iran, and Russia. In evolutionary terms, their species is older than ours, and in the deep past, before humans overtook them and began to relentlessly destroy them, gray wolves were the most widely distributed large predator on the planet. They are also the ancestors of every domestic dog breed. What this implies is that humans and wolves weren't merely *familiar* with each other (the way we're familiar with, say, squirrels), but that we had some kind of intimate and ongoing correspondence—even a series of negotiations that resulted in wolves becoming our pets. Our history, then, is not so much a tale of strangers but of becoming *estranged*.

I'd come to the Fosheim to join three filmmakers, friends of mine, who were making another documentary about Arctic wolves but trying to do it differently by borrowing methods from the biologists who'd studied them. My role was to help them make the film, but I'd also brought questions of my own.

Shortly before I went north I'd had an unsettling first encounter with a wild wolf in a desert city far from home. It had utterly scrambled my view of them. Afterward, I thought of that wolf almost every day. I became more interested in the stories of wolves and in human relationships with them. One consequence of that encounter was that I began to notice the *absence* of wolves everywhere. I was suddenly aware of the old holes left in landscapes and ecosystems by their violent removal. And I saw the results of that legacy in things we took for granted where I lived, on the East Coast of the United States. You could glimpse their goneness in the explosion of the white-tailed deer population, for example. Or in the presence of coyotes on the streets of my parents' Massachusetts suburb. Or in the creeping homogeneity of New England's forests, which could be blamed in part on the deer. These things, now considered *normal*, could be traced directly back to the extermination of wolves during America's centuries-long war against them.

But in the Arctic, far beyond that history, white wolves seemed to have forgotten what humans are capable of. Or perhaps they never knew. It seemed to me they might tell us something—about ourselves and our burning world, maybe even our entangled future. Of course I also wanted to know about the wolves themselves. I had gone most of my life expecting that I would never see one, and I'd never really examined why. The truth is that before my first wolf encounter, I'd come to think of them as nearly imaginary creatures. To see them, you had to believe in them, and mostly I did not.

The Arctic, though, is nothing if not a last refuge of the imagination, and when *National Geographic* invited me to head north and look for wolves, my mind had already been prepared. On the long flight north I stared out the window, watching for ice. When it finally appeared, a bright scatter of broken forms tumbling down the dark velvet sea, I felt myself relax. In our sweltering era, even shattered ice feels like a reprieve. I thought of Admiralty Inlet, where I'd first experienced such ice, and of the narwhals who, so many years before, had opened the way.

WITH A SHOTGUN AND A CAMERA THE BIRD MAN stalked the tundra.

It was 1955, a cold September day, and an American

ornithologist named David Freeland Parmelee was alone, hunting Lapland longspurs on the same plains I would visit almost seventy years later. Longspurs are small songbirds with black masks and rich chestnut napes that migrate to the Arctic during the brief summer to mate and lay their eggs on bare ground. By September most of them have headed south, but a few usually hang around a little longer, eating as much as possible, hedging their bets against the snows that are sure to come soon. Parmelee wanted some of those holdouts—good specimens from the "wildest and northernmost land in all of Canada."

Instead he found white wolves.

At some point in his hunt Parmelee came upon a large musk ox carcass. It was fresh, and he realized that whatever had killed the massive beast was probably still nearby. He turned to find two big white wolves bounding straight for him. One of the wolves veered away but the other rushed on. Parmelee fell to his belly and pointed both his gun and his camera at the wolf, as though uncertain about which sort of shooting to do. Then he came to his senses, ditched the camera, and aimed his gun at the wolf's face.

For some reason—and to me this seems a miracle—Parmelee didn't fire. The wolf stopped a few feet away, and for a moment the two simply looked at each other. Then she approached, sniffing the ground and walking right up to the man. He held the gun ready, but she merely stared, as though she'd never seen anything like him.

This story, recounted by Parmelee years later, is interesting because it seems to be the first detailed description of the Fosheim wolves. Inuit and their ancestors had been traveling over Ellesmere Island for thousands of years prior to Parmelee's arrival and it's possible they knew of the unusual wolves, but I could find no old tales linked to that specific place. Parmelee described the female as *tame*, and even later in his story, after he caught one of her pups, she wasn't aggressive. She merely followed Parmelee back to his camp, whining softly to the pup. When he entered his tent, she waited outside. Parmelee considered bringing the pup home, but her devotion apparently moved him, and eventually he let the pup go.

It wasn't until the mid-1980s that an actual wolf biologist named L. David Mech followed Parmelee's tale to the Fosheim. Mech had been sent, like me, by *National Geographic*, and what he found so startled him that he decided to make Arctic wolves part of his professional focus. He returned for more than twenty summers, and when my friends and I went north in *his* footsteps we borrowed heavily from the work he'd done. This included using four-wheelers to follow the wolves over the rugged earth. By the time I showed up, my companions had been using the machines to keep up with the pack and film their lives for about a month. Just a day after I joined them, I was riding one, too, shadowing wolves over the tundra.

There was no time to acclimate, or worry about how dangerous a four-wheeler could be on unfamiliar terrain. The pack, when we caught up with them, wasn't interested in waiting around. They moved at the speed of life, and, on the tundra this meant fast. Every creature, every plant that had not yet surrendered, was squeezing all it could from the last days of the so-called summer. All knew the transition ahead would be swift. The sun would soon vanish. Winter was a hammer waiting to fall.

That first day was a blur of light and vibration. My teeth rattled and my joints ached as we followed them along frozen riverbeds and over lumpy permafrost, the machine bucking and groaning beneath me. But everything, even the persistent whine of the engine, faded in their presence. Mech had once described it to me like flying, and I finally understood. On foot no human can keep up with a wolf, but the four-wheelers pulled us into the pack's wake.

We followed them down the coast, along stretches of pristine Arctic beach and past rafts of bright ice, then up along ridges covered with white tufts of cotton grass. Turning inland they entered deep green sedge meadows filled, like shrines, with the bleached bones of musk oxen. Hours later they chased giant Arctic hares through mountains white with snow and came down bare sun-washed slopes so steep I had to get off my machine, grip the handlebars, and gently coax it along like a wounded pony, hoping it wouldn't flip and crush me.

The pack's eldest male led them. He was probably the father of the pups and perhaps of the other wolves, too, though my friends had not known the pack long enough to fully understand their relationships. It made sense that they were a family; most packs are. But the life of this little tribe was a book we'd opened at the middle. Their ages, their bloodlines and backstories, even in some cases their genders were unknown to us. The wolf we called Dad often appeared to inhabit the role. His pace was brisk. He ranged without stopping. If the pups lagged behind, and they often did, an older sibling would slip out of line and round them up, nipping at their thighs along the way. It seemed the wolves were searching for musk oxen, following columns of light over the tundra plains and watching for dark shapes in the distance. Now and then the march softened. Dad kept everyone moving, but there was time to sniff at an old bone, or urinate on a lichen-crusted stone. I realized that maybe the pack was hunting *and* teaching, giving the pups a tour of the territory they would soon inherit.

Even in those slower moments the pack never really stopped walking. And the pups, bumbling along at their own pace, took no rest. The wolves seemed untroubled by our presence, and usually I kept a wide distance between the animals and my machine. Sometimes, though, the land funneled us toward each other, or the pack—far surer of their way through fields of boulders and over mound-studded earth—suddenly changed course. Then our paths would cross, braiding together like river channels over a delta. I could hear the growls and whines of the pups then, their ceaseless chatter and in the wolves' fur I could see tiny twigs, mud, and old blood, the grit of summer.

Whenever I neared one of the wolves she would look at me and hold my gaze like no animal I'd ever known. In those moments some truth of what we were trying to do came clear. We had entered their world, more or less on their terms. They were not intimidated but intent on their own plans. Our places, as we usually understand them down south, had been reversed. Now we haunted the edges of *their* lives.

EARLY IN OUR JOURNEY WITH THE PACK, I WAS DRAWN to one wolf, a young female, perhaps three or four years old and maybe forty or fifty pounds. You noticed her right away because she had only one eye. The left had been bashed sideways, the pupil knocked inward. It was no longer visible but stared somewhere into the depths of her skull. What remained was a blank egg-white orb. She was often the wolf who dropped back to gather the pups and was probably their older sister but acted like a kind aunt, encouraging them under Dad's militant pace. Her demeanor, plus her injury, gave her the aura of an underdog, and she had a way of looking at you, cocking her head side to side, *tick-tock, tick-tock,* as though she was trying to read your intentions. The loss of half her sight probably made life harder and reduced her depth perception. It may have reduced her odds of survival, too. But none of that seemed to slow her down.

She was the first wolf to approach me. In one unsettling encounter we were ahead of the wolves and stopped in a dry riverbed to watch them. While the pups rolled along the far bank, the adults veered off their course and loped straight into us. I had been looking at something else—the tundra at my feet, which seemed less soil than a fabric of old bones—when the one-eyed wolf walked up to my machine and nosed around the tailpipe. I looked up and she slowly circled me, nose working, gathering scent, her good eye locked on mine.

I held my breath. I longed to know what she was learning, reading, thinking. From video footage I'd seen earlier, I knew she was the pack's boldest hunter. I'd watched her throw herself into a herd of 400- to 600-pound musk oxen with something that looked like glee. Much later I would see her pull down a big calf by its snout.

I turned my body a few degrees to let her pass. Then I felt a new presence at my back. I pivoted to find the pack's largest wolf, a yearling male, staring into my face. I held still, and then sensed yet another something behind me. It was One Eye. She'd circled back and this time brought her pretty, slightly larger sister. I was suddenly surrounded by wolves.

How easily they'd managed it. How certainly and silently. I felt a thrill I'd never known and a kind of electric heat along my spine. I was shocked to hear their stomachs whingeing and growling. They were hungry, and with glances and flicks of their ears, slight motions of lips and tails, they were communicating. I felt like I was watching people talk in a dream. After a minute or two my heart was racing and I finally broke and spoke to them. Before I could stop myself I realized I was talking as you would to dogs.

The moment collapsed. The wolves dropped their eyes as though they were embarrassed for me. Then they trotted off toward the pups, who had never paused in their tumbleweed procession. They were still headed downcreek, tossing little bones in the air.

MY COMPANIONS AND I FOLLOWED THE PACK FOR twenty-four hours. We did not sleep and stopped only when they did. Once, we watched them attempt to hunt a small herd of musk oxen. But the pack was disorganized, and the oxen were formidable and strong after a summer spent grazing under the midnight sun. One Eye's sister was nearly crushed by a huge bull who rolled her with his loco-motive bulk and dug at her with his meat-hook horns. She escaped, and the hunt collapsed.

At the end of that unbroken day, I was still running on thrill but my body was getting sloppy behind the wheel of my ATV. At one point a tire hit a boulder and I was launched over the handlebars like a circus clown shot from a cannon. On the other side of a wide valley the wolves bedded down below a mountain wall in golden light and numbing cold. The adults curled into their tails while the pups piled together in a downy heap to keep warm. They had caught nothing and would sleep hungry. It occurred to me that, had we been hunters, we might've walked up and shot them all. Wolves down south would never have let us draw so near. These ones seemed to have no idea what we were, or what we might mean.

FEAR GOES BEFORE US LIKE A WAVE.

We spend our days barely aware of the animals flee-ing our footsteps. Squirrels, birds, rats, and stray cats. Raccoons, where I live; coyotes in the backyards of my brothers and parents. Only when animals *don't* run do we tend to notice. When they stake some kind of claim. Then we marvel. If it goes on too long we grow alarmed.

The great attraction of the Fosheim wolves is, of course, that it is possible to be in their close company without feeling the menace usually associated with large predators. That's why anyone visits them. It's why Dave Mech, the wolf biologist, spent years studying them. Once he told me that before he began working on the Fosheim he'd never gotten close to a wild wolf. Only when they'd been caught in a trap or killed had he been able to approach. During the first and longest part of his career he was forced to observe wolves from afar. In places like Michigan and Minnesota, Alaska and elsewhere, he had to spot them with scopes and use radio collars to plot their movements.

Mech began studying wolves in the late 1950s, which coincided with the last phases of the American war on them. By then it had been going on since the colonial era, a campaign of some four hundred years that echoes in its violence and relentlessness the genocide of Native Americans. White settlers used any means at their disposal to rid the landscape of things they perceived to be impediments to progress or prosperity. When Mech was studying for his Ph.D., there were almost no wolves left to kill in the Lower 48. They hung on in certain pockets of the mountain west and in the remote Midwest, near Canada, but these were fugitive populations, traumatized and wary.

The extermination of wolves was driven by a lot of things, including colonialism and capitalism—the same forces still at work all over the world, eating what's left, digging for more, denying the entangled crises of climate and extinction. European colonists carried with them to North America a special dread of wolves that you can still recognize in folktales and religious art. Wolves were sometimes seen as servants of Satan, or of witches. They were said to embody many of the worst qualities that humans recognized in themselves, including greed, malice, and gluttony. You can glimpse strains of that old antipathy in the modern politicization of wolves, particularly in the West, where efforts to return them to various landscapes or protect them from hunters are deeply, sometimes virulently, controversial. Wolves have become both an animal and a line to be crossed. You can be for or against them. Perhaps, after centuries of killing, this is what progress now looks like.

Like Mech, I was born into the aftermath of the wolf wars. I grew up in Massachusetts in the 1980s, where wolves had been killed off the landscape some hundred and fifty years earlier. Historical documents show that the first wolf bounties in the New World were offered just south of my hometown. No one I knew in childhood really feared wolves, except in abstract or perhaps instinctual ways, as you might recoil from a snake. My brothers and I roamed abandoned farmland, silent empty forests, and crumbling mill yards without a thought of wolves.

By then they had become an endangered species and the slow rehabilitation of their story had begun. When I was in college, in the mid-1990s, the animals were reintroduced to Yellowstone National Park, where they'd been exterminated less than a century before. The park today has become a kind of living laboratory for wolf research, the largest in the world. But most Americans of my generation have lived their entire lives without seeing or hearing a wolf. Most never will.

I was forty before I saw one. This was the encounter that had changed me. It was in Kirkuk, an ancient city in northern Iraq, where I had gone to report on the war against the Islamic State. One day while walking below the city's ancient citadel I came to a shop selling exotic-animals. Ostriches sat outside in the swelter, their black feathers dull with dust. There was a huge tortoise. Some kind of antelope. A rotund aquatic mammal. Tired of thinking about the war, I went in.

The shop was a madhouse—shrieking, barking, singing, gnawing animals packed into cages and tanks. I saw monkeys, bright-plumed birds, turtles of many kinds, and, in small glass jars, actual legless lizards. At the back, in a heavy steel cage lay a wolf. The shopkeeper's son appeared out of the noise to tell me he'd been captured in Iran and hauled over the border.

"Who would buy a wolf?" I asked, incredulous.

"A rich man," he said.

"Why?"

He shrugged.

The wolf watched me without moving. That steady gaze I would see a couple years later on the Fosheim Peninsula. In his cage he reminded me of Islamic State fighters I had interviewed, boys barely twenty who'd been captured trying to sneak back into the city to visit their families and would soon be executed. I thought of widows I'd met, of parents who'd lost children and children who'd lost limbs, whole communities shattered. Somehow in the wolf's silence these details of suffering welled up, and there in the shop I nearly wept.

Suddenly I remembered that in that city *I* was a rich man. I reached into my pocket, felt a roll of sweaty bills. For $500 the wolf could be mine. I had enough, I could buy him and maybe an ostrich, too. My employer would never know. I could borrow a car. Smile my way through the checkpoints. I could drive east into the mountains over the minefields and release the wolf back into Iran. I had no idea what I'd do with the ostrich.

The shopkeeper's son recognized the look on my face. He stepped behind the counter and pulled down a leash and a black leather muzzle.

"Take these, too," he said.

But I walked away. I told myself there was nothing I could do.

AT THE TOP OF A HILL NOT FAR FROM OUR CAMP THERE IS a wolf den. Most dens aren't much to look at—little more than shallow scrapes in the soil. This one lies within an outcrop of tea-colored sandstone that looks in profile like a great hook-beaked gargoyle. The gargoyle crouches on the tundra, facing east, and in its heart is a small natural cave. Wolf mothers use dens only for a short time and leave them soon after pups are born, but in this frozen country a good den can be hard to find and this one has become an heirloom. Years ago Dave Mech observed wolves using the den, and the broad skirt of oxen bones scattered around it is another testament to its longevity. I visit a couple of times and crawl inside. Floor of pale sand, smooth dark walls. The silence of a church. To enter the rock is to be embraced. Sitting at the cave mouth, looking out over the vast plains, you feel omniscient: nothing is hidden from view. You can imagine the generations born here, a steady procession of pups tumbling out, dopey and drooling, into the Arctic light.

To such dens pregnant wolves retreat in early spring and usually deliver sometime in June. Pups are born blind. When their eyes first open they are blue, and later they turn brown. After several weeks the pups emerge, often into the company of older brothers and sisters and sometimes uncles and aunts who've been waiting to meet them. Pack life then arranges itself around the pups who must, Mech reminded me several times, be *taught* how to be wolves—how to hunt and stalk, how to travel and cooperate. Wolf families were once thought to be arranged in stiff hierarchies that were decided by competition and violence. At the top an alpha pair was thought to rule—a male and female who won the right to breed and demanded submission from the rest of the pack. They dominated pack life according to some canid version of the law of the jungle.

This concept of alpha wolves reigned among biologists for so long and seemed so accurate that like a virus it jumped species into our own culture. You've probably heard it used by a self-described alpha male or female, someone who considers themselves to be a leader, a winner, successful in business or the bedroom. Someone who gets what they want. As a mid-career researcher Mech helped popularize the idea in a book he wrote about wolves. He didn't mean to, and told me many times he regretted the way it passed into human pop culture and became annoying, then ridiculous.

Mech said the concept originated in the 1930s and '40s, when researchers couldn't actually get close to wolves because there were so few left. The scholarship that gave rise to the alpha model came from a study of captive wolves—a random assortment of individuals who were tossed together in a small enclosure at a zoo in Basel. They were strangers, not family, and they fought, threatened, and tried to dominate each other.

The limitations of that study appear clear to us now. Several biologists have likened it to cramming a bunch of prison inmates together in a cell and then trying to craft grand theories about human behavior from the results. But the theory didn't die until Mech came to the Arctic. After a decade or so spent with the wolves on the Fosheim he realized the alpha model was wrong, that the alpha wolf didn't really exist. Wild wolves simply don't behave that way, he told me. We understand now that wolf families are much more like our own: often headed by a mother and father, a breeding pair, who are surrounded by their children from successive years. There may be some sort of dominance in a wolf pack, Mech said, but it's a natural sort of order, where the parents are in charge. The whole power-struggle thing was a myth. It was humans once more casting themselves over creation.

What this story offers is a sense of the Arctic's remove, and the singular value of its wildness. The tundra allows you to see things that simply aren't visible anywhere else. From within the stone embrace of a wolf den, the view opens uncluttered before you. Sitting in that space where so many wolves had been born, I think of the alpha myth and its drift into our own culture, where the term usually seems to be applied to men. This makes a certain kind of sense, in societies that are deeply patriarchal. But wolves are not that way. Mech told me his observations suggested that female wolves, matriarchs, often seemed to be making many, if not most, of a given pack's decisions. On the Fosheim that's what the filmmakers had seen, too. The pack's matriarch, an older female with a thick ruff, had been formidable. She was the obvious center of the family, right up until she disappeared.

IT HAPPENED JUST BEFORE I ARRIVED. ONE DAY, AFTER following the wolves for a while, my friends had separated from the pack to rest and refuel. When they returned they found only nine wolves. They never saw the matriarch again.

I was at home in New York when I got an email from one of the filmmakers about her disappearance.

"They're messed up," my friend wrote of the pack. "She was the most important member and without her, no one quite seems to know what to do."

At the time I didn't know much about the matriarch, and as soon as I reached the Fosheim I sat in a tent with my friends, watching on a laptop footage taken of her while she'd been alive. You see in the video files that she appears thin. She walks with a limp and along her chest there is a shadowy ripple of ribs. She'd given birth to the pups probably in June and spent the rest of her life feeding and educating them. Shortly before she vanished she had helped her family take down a young musk ox. Then she kept all the other wolves away from the carcass and allowed only the pups to feed. When her older children approached, she bared her teeth in warning. They whined and begged, but she held firm. The pups were vulnerable. They needed the meat most.

I watched this scene many times and I could not help thinking that she knew what was coming. The pups had only recently been weaned and she served them this final meal of solid food, cementing their connection to oxen, to the source they would rely on forever after. But I think she must have been trying to impart something to her older children, too. She was showing them how to care for their younger brothers and sisters. It's hard to know if they took the lesson. Later, when I watched the pack kill a musk ox after days or perhaps weeks without much food, the pups had to fend for themselves against their much bigger siblings.

From what I could gather the matriarch had always set the tone for the pack. With my friends she held herself aloof, neither fearful nor particularly interested. How she learned to be this way around humans was unknown, though she may have been related to wolves that Mech had studied, even to the so-called *tame* wolf that the bumbling ornithologist, Parmelee, had met in the 1950s. This is to say her tolerance for humans may have been an heirloom. Knowledge passed down in the same way she'd tried, before her death, to teach her older children to care for her younger ones.

Now that she was gone the wolves had entered a new phase of life. The filmmakers could not say whether or how the pack mourned, but it's reasonable to believe they did, in their own ways. Biologists have observed that wolf packs can splinter after a matriarch's death. Wolves drift away, search for new mates, new families. Sometimes wolves die when their families crumble.

The most obvious fallout for the Fosheim wolves seemed to be that they were no longer able to hunt effectively. They weren't sure who to follow. Dad wolf appeared at times to be trying to lead. And One Eye's older sister—the one who'd been nearly gored and trampled by an ox—seemed to be newly assertive, as though she wanted to fill her mother's space.

Like any human family, the wolves had been scrambled by the death of their mother. During my final days with them I thought a lot about this, and how much we humans are so thoroughly tethered to the stories of our parents, even if we don't know them well, or at all. Like strands in a rope our lives are woven together with those of our families, our ancestors, with stories so distant we can no longer see them, though we may still feel their pull. How did the weaving happen among wolves? How might it be undone, or damaged, or healed? Now that the matriarch was gone, who would care for the pups? Who would be next to use the family's den and lie, perhaps, where she had lain?

ALL OF THIS WAS ON MY MIND ONE EVENING WHEN I went out looking for the wolves. It was the second week of September, my time on Ellesmere was closing, and I wanted to be alone with them. I drove in the direction where they'd last been seen and came to a place where the land formed a large bowl. At the bottom, a herd of fifteen musk oxen lay on the dead grass while a solitary bull stood among them, staring at me. It was twenty-five degrees. In the weak light they looked like boulders, ancient, inert, unmovable. Lumps of raw matter hurled up on the shore of time. I was pleased because oxen always eventually attract wolves. All I needed to do was wait.

It wasn't long before I turned and saw a white form on a distant ridge. I'd been fooled by white rocks and ghostly owls and the big Arctic hares before, but then the form began to howl. I howled, too, and then others, invisible to me, joined in. The hills were howling. I drove slowly toward the form. It waited. When I was close I saw it was One Eye's sister. She trotted a little distance to the crest of a hill where she paused and looked over her shoulder. I caught up and together we went down. Before I sank below the crest I looked back toward the ox, the sentry, but he'd joined the others on the ground and become one among the lumps.

The wolf and I crossed a few low hills. In a drainage we found another wolf, rolling and rubbing around on the bare bones of a musk ox. It was One Eye. The sisters greeted each other, One Eye submissive, licking and whining softly, and then they were off. The wolves walked side by side, shoulder to shoulder. They drifted over pebbled hilltops and across struggling skirts of grass where the blades were stiff with ice. The country all around had turned purple in twilight. I felt a boyish sort of joy, less charged than the thrill of our first day together. I wanted nothing but to be with them, to go wherever they were going.

Now and then the sisters paused and I caught up and we carried on. I understood they were leading me somewhere, and over the next hill I saw it: Below, beside a small frozen pond, the rest of the family was waiting. Already I could see their excitement. Their tails waving like bright flags in a wind.

FOR MORE THAN A DAY I SAT WITH THE PACK BY THE pond. Mostly I kept still, for the simple reason that I did not want to interrupt their joy. Any movement on my part attracted attention and broke the rhythm of whatever they were doing. To sit and freeze and watch was enough, though eventually I was forced to stand and run in place, or wing my arms in circles to force blood back out into aching fingers. When the shivering stopped I sat again and settled in to wait, into wolf time.

During those hours the sun wobbled low around the horizon, moving through phases of dusk. The light was purple and the pond opalescent, a dark mirror of the universe. To the east the plains rolled unbroken toward snow-dusted mountains. Westward the earth rose into bare, rock-stubbled hills. In the strange Arctic light that neither followed sunset nor promised dawn, the tundra seemed open and endless, a world without shadows. Something you might walk across forever.

I observed hours passing in the number of words I scratched into my notebook. The wolves lounged. They rotated through activities, like kids at an amusement park. There was a game of keep-away on the pond, where they played for a couple of hours with an ice puck, slipping, slapping, and scrabbling until finally the largest pup, that potbellied bully, decided he'd had enough. He stole the puck and chomped it to pieces. Napping happened in a patch of thick grass to the east. And then there was the feeding station, at the carcass of a musk ox, which was flipped over and stripped bare as a stolen car. In the hulk of its body the wolves dug for scraps, twisting hide, pulling sinew. Wrestling over the least bits. They were hungry. One Eye cracked bones between her teeth.

Two wolves—dad wolf and a slender-footed female who seemed to be another daughter—showed no interest in me and kept well away. The rest ebbed and flowed, approaching me, retreating, coming forward with questions of their own. In these moments the wolves drew so near I could count the twigs in their fur, see how the colors of their eyes ranged from coffee to hazel to a luminous gold. There was also the grub-white of One Eye's ruined orb. I wanted to ask if the injury had hurt, if it hurt her still. Once or twice she came and stood beside me, inspecting me, *tick-tock, tick-tock*. Her good eye, I noticed was copper brown. In her hair were strands of gray. It seemed to me she was asking why I had come, and what I hoped to learn.

Hours later, while I chipped a hole in the pond ice to draw water, One Eye concealed herself in the folds of the tundra and crept up to my tent. The other wolves had gathered around me at the pond's edge, like students attending a lecture. I realized at some point that One Eye was not among them and I looked up to see my tent flapping wildly in the wind. But there was no wind.

She'd sliced open the nylon skin of the tent with alarming precision, separating by some means the floor from the wall exactly along the seam. Then she hauled out all my stuff and arranged it neatly on the grass. She selected for her trophy my inflatable pillow and waited with it in her mouth until I reached her. Then she ran off, tail high, lips pulled back around the pillow in something like a grin.

I was furious, and without thinking I began to chase her. Then I stopped. This was what she wanted. She was testing me. As she bounded away, my anger evaporated and all I could do was laugh.

Most of our last hours together were spent sleeping. Or, I should say, the wolves slept. Now and then one of them startled herself awake, looked around, caught my gaze and held it. Then she folded herself back down and covered her snout with her tail. Soon she was chasing something through a dream. These are the moments I myself will dream of, years from now and in other parts of the Arctic. At one point, nonsensical with cold, I found myself counting the sleeping wolves again and again, as though they were sheep in a nursery rhyme. *Nine white wolves on the dark brown earth*, a line I would one day repeat to my young sons, in the warm den of their room. In this way they will slowly come to consider the wolves a story, and my journey with them a kind of myth. They are not wrong to do so. As years have passed, I have often wondered what of that time was true.

Eventually the adults woke, followed by the pups, and the family greeted each other in their intensely happy way. Soon the older wolves left me with the pups, and we had our bumbling adventure together. After the pack reunited, I kept following them and met up with one of the filmmakers. Together we stayed with the pack for hours more, watching as they finally managed to hunt and kill a musk oxen calf.

The hunt was violent and swift, a twilit blur of feet and fur. I recall how the calf's herd eventually abandoned her and thundered away. She cried after them, and bleated desperately as the wolves closed in. Finally One Eye fastened her teeth to the calf's snout and hauled her down. The calf's death was terrifying, though it also showed the pack had sorted themselves out—they had not been broken by their mother's death. In the hunt's aftermath, One Eye's sister strode onto the frost-lined tundra and gave a series of long triumphant howls. Her coat was slick with ox blood. She stood with her shoulders squared against the world. The hunt had changed something, and it seemed clear this wolf had risen into some new authority. But we would never see what it meant for the rest of the family. Not long after, my friends and I gathered our gear and flew home, leaving the story of their lives where we'd found it, somewhere in the middle.

It has now been several years since I returned to my life in the south, and I think of the wolves each day. Sometimes my thoughts seem to pick up midstream, as though I were still sitting at the frozen pond, in silent conversation with them. Questions occur to me now that I was never able to ask, that I did not even consider back then. I also realize how much of my time with the wolves was spent in a trance, watching and reacting, absorbing and searching. Sometimes I fear I may have lost whatever I learned from them, that my memory of our wordless hours are being backfilled with meaningless southern noise. But in quiet moments some of the lessons return. What I remember most clearly is trust. How the wolves felt safe enough in my presence to sleep, and to dream. How they were content to leave their children in my company, if not my care, and let us wander into the cold.

# NORTHWEST PASSAGES

*Qikiktaq / King William Island*

WHEN ROALD AMUNDSEN REACHED THE south coast of King William Island, Canada in September 1903, no one was there to greet him. The Norwegian explorer may have been disappointed—he'd hoped to meet the Inuit—but he was also patient, and perhaps he guessed that the Inuit would eventually find him. He put his ship, a converted trawler called *Gjøa*, into a snug natural harbor and settled in to wait. His immediate plan was to let the sea freeze around the *Gjøa*. His larger goal was to become the first to sail through the Northwest Passage, which European explorers had been trying, failing, and dying to do for nearly four hundred years. Beyond that he had even broader ambitions, and for these Amundsen knew he needed help from the locals.

Several weeks later, at the end of October, a small band

of hunters from a tribe called Netsilingmiut, "the people of the seal," appeared on the shore above the harbor. They had earlier spotted the ship but had been hesitant to approach, for while they'd probably heard stories of Europeans, it does not seem that any in the group had actually seen one before. The hunters consulted a shaman, an *angakok*, who convinced them to visit the white men, and when they finally approached, an equally nervous Amundsen walked out to greet them.

Soon the two groups were on good terms. They traded, visited, tried to communicate. Slowly the Norwegians picked up some of the Netsilingmiut language, which is a dialect of Inuktitut, and they learned that the name of the harbor where they'd anchored was *Uqsuqtuq*, which means "there's a lot of fat there," a reference to abundant marine mammals. The Netsilingmiut, for their part, came to call Amundsen "Amusi with the big nose," after his most formidable physical feature.

The Norwegians would stay for almost two years. During their sojourn they made measurements of the Earth's magnetic field and eventually fixed the location of the North Magnetic Pole. They also learned from the Netsilingmiut how to survive in the Arctic—how to build igloos, drive sleds, handle sled dogs. Perhaps most important of all they learned how to properly dress in clothing made of caribou hide.

In August 1905, after the ice had melted sufficiently to free the *Gjøa*, Amundsen slipped out of the harbor and sailed west, into the last portion of the Passage that had never been sailed by white men. Five years after that, he sailed to Antarctica, where he became the first to reach the South Pole. With this success, Amundsen became the greatest living explorer, and in photographs taken there at the bottom of the world, you understand what he owed to the Netsilingmiut at the top: He and his men are dressed in pants and parkas sewn of caribou hide. Sleds and dogs surround them in the snow. They look like hunters. They look like the people of the seal.

MARVIN ATQITTUQ GREW UP IN GJOA HAVEN, THE town that sprang from Amundsen's visit, and he knew all the stories. You couldn't live there and *not* know them. Even after more than a century it was impossible to escape the explorer's shadow. He was there in the little museum, where some of his artifacts lay in glass cases. He was there in a memorial, high above town, which was dedicated to the centuries-long quest for the Northwest Passage. He was there, of course, in the name of the town itself, taken from his ship. And in the foyer of the town hall there sat a massive bronze bust of the Norwegian, greeting every visitor, his inimitable nose rubbed to gleaming by a steady stream of inquisitive hands.

Amundsen's ghost even haunted people's memories. His story had been passed down in oral accounts by relatives of the people who'd met him. For a long time one of Marvin's neighbors, a man named Paul Ikuallaq, had believed he was related to Amundsen by blood, though a DNA test eventually silenced that tale. Even the few tourists who reached this part of the Arctic came hoping to briefly bask in the explorer's aura, and see a place where Arctic history had been made.

Marvin was twenty-seven, and in his life so far he'd passed through various stages of relationship to Amundsen and other European explorers, from a schoolboy's pale interest to a young man's irritation at the way they soaked up so much light. Recently he was simply over it. He'd stopped caring about Amusi with the big nose and all the others who had trekked through his backyard on their Passage quests. Their stories didn't have much to offer. Their achievements and tragedies did not speak to him.

This was the state in which I met Marvin, on a frigid night in late November at the community center in Gjoa Haven. A meeting of the local militia had been convened, and Marvin and his father, Jacob, were members. I'd come to spend time with the militia, called the Canadian Rangers, and that night they were holding a snap election to choose a new leader. I walked across town through a slow-rolling snowstorm to observe.

In a cavernous room, twenty or so Rangers had gathered, wearing the bright red hoodies and ball caps that were their official government-issue uniform. Creak of folding chairs, squeak of wet boots on a hard plastic floor. Here and there I skirted a soft conversation in Inuktitut. I took a seat along the edge of the room, looked up, and saw Amundsen, who stared down from a large mounted photograph.

The Rangers are a volunteer reserve force attached to the Canadian army. Their units can be found all across the north, usually in small towns like Gjoa Haven, places where you could walk out your back door and disappear, if you wished, into the nation's vast uninhabited wildernesses. In a way, Ranger units are an answer to all that space. The regular Canadian military is very small relative to the enormity of the country itself, and there is no practical way its forces can occupy or even patrol its northern landscapes. Here the Rangers step in, and they operate something like a frontier guard crossed with a fish-and-game club. From their isolated communities they run occasional patrols into the backcountry, and they assist the military with cold-weather survival training and search-and-rescue operations. More rarely they participate in war games, where they play scouts in the sorts of scenarios that imagine an enemy—usually Russia—invading over the top of the globe. Many Rangers are recruited from local Indigenous groups, and in Gjoa Haven all of them were Inuit. Down south, in the provinces where most Canadians live, the Rangers are often called "the eyes and ears in the north."

Marvin and Jacob Atqittuq had been Rangers for years. I would learn that, like many of their comrades, they'd joined for various reasons, including the pay you received while on missions and the supplies of ammunition, gasoline, and equipment handed out by the army. There was also, among the Atqittuqs and most of the other Rangers, a certain regard for country. This wasn't to say that any of them felt particularly loyal to the federal government in Ottawa, or even to the Inuit-led government of their own territory, Nunavut. It was lost on no one that by joining the Rangers they were agreeing to keep watch over territory that had been taken from them generations earlier and folded into the settler state called Canada.

What Gjoa Haven's Rangers shared, though, was a love of *nuna*, that Inuit concept of land and belonging that included the earth and the sea and everything within, especially the animals. Most of the Rangers simply desired to be out in *nuna* and near animals as much as possible. Modern life didn't necessarily make that easy. Even in Gjoa Haven, some two thousand miles north of the Canadian capital, the gravity of modern life, of school and work, could be as relentless as anywhere else. The Ranger corps offered one way, however complicated, to keep modern life at bay. It allowed many of the Rangers to be out on the land more often.

Another part of the allure was that there wasn't much of a martial dimension to the Ranger program. It was far more casual than a national guard. I saw no actual interest in warfare or combat or any of the other aspects of soldiering that commonly draw people into militia down south. There was also little real hierarchy beyond the elected commander, and all of this made things less organized but more nimble. In the community center that night the election moved swiftly. The crowd nominated three candidates, and Marvin, tall and broad-shouldered, was the youngest by a couple of decades. Votes were written on scraps of paper, tossed into a hat. A sergeant from the army tallied them up. There was applause when Marvin won, but he just looked stunned, like a man ambushed. Later, outside in the snow, I caught up with him and his father while they warmed up their snowmobiles for the short drive home. I asked Marvin how he felt about his new job and his face went blank.

"Not good!" he said. "I voted for the other guy."

One of the many responsibilities Marvin had suddenly inherited was the Rangers' next patrol, which would leave in a couple of days. The group had not yet decided where exactly they would travel—King William Island is about the size of the state of Connecticut, and Gjoa Haven is its only town. But due to the island's place at the middle of the Northwest Passage, they would almost certainly travel along it, and in some way I thought they would be in conversation with it. This was something I wanted to hear.

I asked Marvin if I could join him, and a look of shock shot across his face, same as the moment he realized he'd been elected to lead the Rangers. Behind us Jacob said, "Oh shit!" And then he laughed himself nearly to tears.

We said good night, and the Atqittuqs cruised along Gjoa's empty streets toward the small single-story home they shared with their families. On the way they could see the frozen harbor where Amundsen had anchored the *Gjoa*. They passed the museum where his relics were kept and the town hall where the bronze bust slept. At the foot of town father and son could even make out a section of the Passage itself, that once-great prize, the most sought-after shipping route in history. It lay frozen and blank and faintly aglow in the town-light, just a few doors down from their house.

KING WILLIAM ISLAND SITS AT THE BOTTOM OF THE Canadian Arctic Archipelago, a constellation of some thirty-six thousand islands that gradually gathers toward the North Pole. This was the expanse that European explorers had spent centuries trying to navigate. It was the riddle Amundsen had finally solved. The region is more than twice the size of France, but across it are scattered only about twenty thousand people; fewer, in other words, than you could find in a minor Parisian suburb.

The island's position makes Gjoa Haven one of Canada's remotest human enclaves. The nearest neighboring community is Taloyoak, about a hundred miles east across the sea. The next nearest is Cambridge Bay, two hundred and thirty miles to the west, on another island. Directly south, across a narrow strait, are the Canadian barren lands. In its isolation, Gjoa Haven is like every other town in the territory of Nunavut, and whatever arrives here, from bullets and Bibles to diapers and diesel fuel and virtually everything else, comes by air or aboard the cargo ship that visits once each summer, if the weather and the ice allow.

The first time I visited Gjoa, in 2017, it had just two stores and no service sector. There were no dentists or mechanics. No pharmacies or coffee shops. Amazon did not deliver and the regular mail was spotty. There were no bars and no restaurants, unless you counted the one in Gjoa's only hotel, which catered almost exclusively to the kind of white people (scientists, contractors, politicians, me) who circulated through the north like odd migratory birds.

When it came to simple things, Marvin said, they were simply hard in Gjoa Haven. He told me this a couple of days after the election. We were rattling around town in a battered pickup, running errands. Among the most noticeably absent things in town, he said, were barbers and doctors. He ran a hand over his own short black hair and said he'd done it himself, just as he'd buzzed the heads of his dad and his young son. Suddenly I understood why every man I'd met had the same haircut. And so it was with nearly all of life's basic procedures: You either went DIY, or you let things slide. In the best cases you waited until you flew down south to a big town, like Yellowknife, in the Northwest Territories. Almost everyone I met had traveled there at some point, usually to see a doctor or get a tooth pulled. During the trip, people told me, they often tried to fit in a trim.

The isolation didn't usually bother Marvin. He did not feel as though he was missing out or disconnected from the broader Canadian culture. Occasionally, though, something happened, or did not happen, that framed the distance between Gjoa Haven and the south in glaring relief. When we met, Marvin was particularly vexed by the lack of mobile phone service, which had not yet reached the island. Phones are a measure of worth and wealth everywhere—so ubiquitous now that it's strange to meet someone who doesn't have one. This was no less true in the far north, and like all his friends Marvin owned a phone anyway. It was a kind of aspirational accessory. Useful, sometimes, when he traveled south. But lately the fact that it didn't work in his hometown was a reminder to Marvin of exactly who and where he was: last on the list for services most other Canadians could take for granted.

At one point he tapped his phone, which sat on the console between us, and said, "Kinda sucks that I can't call a doctor if my kid's sick."

"But there aren't any doctors here anyway?" I said.

"Oh yeah!!" Marvin grinned. "I forgot."

ONE OF MARVIN'S FIRST ACTS AS COMMANDER WAS to preside over a vote on where the Rangers would make their patrol. There were, apparently, two options. They might drive their snowmobiles deep into the island's interior, or stick closer to the coast, where, I was told, it was slightly warmer. At that time of year, when autumn, *ukiaq*, was transitioning into winter, *ukiuk*, brutal winds hurtled down over King William, and there was almost nothing in the way of topography to stop or mitigate them. What this meant in practical terms was that each day the temperature seemed to fall a little farther, as the days grew shorter. By early December the sun would sink below the horizon and not rise again for a month.

The Rangers picked the route nearer the coast, which meant we would parallel the part of the Passage that followed the island's eastern shore. Our route would take us almost directly north of town to a lake called Kakivaktorvik. There, Marvin would lead the platoon through a week of martial exercises, including GPS training, target practice, and search-and-rescue scenarios. Plenty of time would also be set aside for hunting and fishing. Kakivaktorvik was an old word that meant "place to fish with a spear." No one used spears anymore, but Marvin assured me everyone would bring a net.

Ranger patrols, I had learned, almost always incorporate hunting and fishing, and this was because many people in remote northern communities still rely on those practices to supplement their income and fill their refrigerators. This was uniquely true in the Arctic, where subsistence, and the traditional skills required to be good at it, were still practiced widely. Southern military leaders had long ago realized they couldn't expect people to volunteer for service if it would keep them from making a living, so the army built the old ways into the program. It even provided each Ranger with a rifle—a heavy bolt-action Lee-Enfield, leftover from the Second World War.

In Gjoa Haven, members of the Ranger platoon were busy organizing their gear, packing up everything they'd need for a week on the land in sub-zero conditions. They were also inspecting their snowmobile tracks and engines, adding low-viscosity oil, making sure things were in order from headlights to the tiny heaters on thumb throttles, a blessing of technology that could help prevent frostbite while you drove through the cold. Marvin circled through town, checking in with people, helping them find parts, delivering supplies. He was naturally good at this and had an easy rapport with the other Rangers. Everyone seemed to understand that he hadn't actually wanted the commander's job. Everyone also knew it wasn't the sort of thing he could refuse.

Several of the Rangers were older, in their late fifties and sixties, and Marvin's father was the oldest of all, at seventy-three. I noticed that with these men, Marvin tended to speak in Inuktitut, something he never did with Rangers closer to his own age. He told me that with certain subjects, it was easier for the men to speak their first

language. When I asked about the younger guys, he just
said, "None of them really speaks it."

Language set Marvin apart. In small towns across the
Arctic, fluency in Inuktitut and other Indigenous languages was fading. There were many reasons for this, but
what crouched at the bottom of it all, as with almost every
challenge in the north, was colonialism. During the late
nineteenth century and up to the middle of the twentieth, generations of Indigenous children in Canada and the
United States had been sent to residential schools where
they were forbidden to speak their native tongues. In Arctic Canada, those children grew up to be the grandparents
and parents of Marvin's generation. They could not pass
down language because it simply wasn't there: It had been
stolen from them years before.

Within this context, Marvin's story was doubly unusual. Not only had his parents taught him Inuktitut, but
Jacob and his wife, Martha, hardly spoke any English at all.
Martha sang in her church choir from an Inuktitut hymn-
book. Jacob knew a few English phrases and he mostly
used them to make jokes. He loved to say *Goddammit!* and
then laugh at the sonic silliness of the phrase. He used his
own language for whatever was actually worth discussing.
When I asked how this had happened, how they'd managed to come this far without drowning in English, Marvin
grinned and said, "Igloo times."

His parents had been born in the 1940s, far to the
southeast, on the Canadian mainland. Their people were
called Utkuhiksalingmiut, which means, loosely, "the people of the place where there is soapstone." They lived along

what is now called the Back River in a roadless, townless, virtually inaccessible landscape, and there they were semi-nomadic hunters and fishers. In winter they traveled by dogsled, in summer they went overland on foot, their dogs following along wearing little leather packs of their own.

The Utkuhiksalingmiut lived in such isolation that in the 1960s an American anthropologist named Jean Briggs went north to live with them, hoping she would find the last surviving strains of the old faith, the religion of shamans, spirits, and magic. But Briggs was too late. She arrived in Jacob's community to find everyone was Anglican.

But while the missionaries had managed to erase traditional faith, the Utku, as Briggs called them, resisted other changes. In the late 1950s and early '60s, for example, Jacob and other Utku hunters routinely sledded north to Gjoa Haven in the winter, where they traded hides and fish for ammunition, tea, sugar, and other supplies. The men observed town life and recognized the harm it might cause. They saw traditional life dissolving, people estranged from the land, children schooled in English. Utku children were beginning to be sent to residential schools at the time, but Briggs described how they would return to the Back River in summer to be with their families.

Jacob would later tell me that he and Martha had moved to Gjoa Haven reluctantly, in the late 1960s. I was not certain whether the government had coerced the couple and their community into leaving—as had happened before, to other Inuit groups—or if they'd had their own reasons. Jacob's and Martha's older son, Tommy, eventually began to attend school in the town and the couple didn't want to abandon the boy to the system they'd spent so long avoiding. "We didn't want him to cry for missing us," Jacob told me.

From what I could piece together of that time, the Atqittuqs were among the last of the semi-nomadic hunters to leave the land. After their departure, the tundra began to slowly close over their old camps, and a deeper, colder kind of emptiness descended.

WHEN I MET JACOB HE STILL LIVED AS MUCH AS HE could by the old ways. He remained a formidable hunter—a man who was said to have once caught a killer whale by himself down in Hudson Bay—and he often went out alone, stalking seals over the frozen sea. He took a rifle and a harpoon, wore the parka Martha had sewn for him. No one ever worried about whether or not he would return. At home, he and Martha made sure Marvin grew up speaking an Inuktitut inflected with the peculiar dialect of their own people.

In this way, Marvin was linked to the igloo times by threads of language and memory. Even if he hadn't known them personally, even if those days had long since passed away, he still lived at their margins. He was a conduit, a messenger standing at a threshold, and he was often called upon to translate, to explain, to play liaison between generations. Later, several of the older Rangers told me this was exactly why they'd elected him to lead. He could speak Inuktitut. He understood tradition. With his father behind him he was moored in what mattered most.

AT A CERTAIN POINT DURING OUR RAMBLE AROUND town, I asked Marvin about climate change. We were sitting outside one of Gjoa Haven's two stores, watching a couple of kids play in a snowbank. A frigid wind pushed in from the frozen sea and it'd dropped the temperature to around twenty degrees below zero. Marvin turned up the truck's heater, which poured hot noise into our laps.

Part of my reason for coming to Gjoa Haven was to learn about Arctic warming from Inuit perspectives, and especially to see how climate transformation was unfolding at the center of the Northwest Passage. A few months before I arrived, in late August, a Chinese icebreaker named *Xue Long*, which means Snow Dragon, entered the Passage from the east, using Davis Strait. The ship's voyage caused a stir in Toronto and Washington, D.C., for it was read as a declaration of Chinese interest in the warming north. That interest wasn't actually new; China had previously announced itself a "near-Arctic state," and said it would pursue its own interests in the Arctic wherever international law allowed. Nor was the icebreaker's voyage a surprise: China had told Canada in advance that the ship was coming. But the reaction was briefly intense, and it was used by some politicians to claim that Canada wasn't paying enough attention to the far north.

The Northwest Passage is actually a composite: not one route, but several possible paths through the labyrinth of the Arctic Archipelago. Most ships cruise over the top of King William Island, while some sail around it, like Amundsen did, and proceed along the southern shore. As one set of "eyes and ears in the north," part of Marvin's job was occasionally to observe passing ships, or at least be *ready* to. To him the *Xue Long*'s transit through the Passage was no big deal. After all, it was just one ship.

By that point, the thick barrier of polar sea ice that had kept ships out of the Passage for centuries had been shrinking at astonishing rates for a decade. Almost every summer seemed to set or threaten a new record for ice loss, and among the many consequences was that shipping companies now eyeing the Passage with fresh interest. That summer, the *Xue Long* was merely one of the last ships in a procession of thirty-three that successfully navigated the Passage, including tankers, freighters, passenger ships, and several private yachts. Never before had this many ships come through in a single season. The next year sea ice would return and clot the Passage again, allowing only a handful of ships through. The trend, though, appeared clear: by the end of 2023, forty-one ships would transit the Passage; 2024 would see thirty-eight.

The traffic, I thought, would've made Amundsen's head spin. Merchants had been dreaming of an ice-free route over the top of the globe since the Middle Ages, and dozens of expeditions had gone north in search of one. But the frozen sea had always ruined their plans. By 1905, when the Norwegians finally completed the Passage, most other explorers, navies, and merchants had given up hope that it would ever become a useful sea road. It was too dangerous, too cold, too choked with ice. Amundsen's slow journey only seemed to confirm this, and after him no one bothered to sail the Passage for almost fifty years.

In the news that autumn, just before I flew to King

William Island, the parade of vessels had been reported with alarm but also a kind of excitement. To some it was a sign of worsening climate crisis; to others it was denouement— the old European dream finally coming true. For Marvin, the most noticeable change was that tourists now arrived in town. Their presence in Gjoa was one way you could measure the larger shift in the Arctic. Beyond that, Marvin didn't think this modern traffic was very different from the old kind. Ships arrived, departed, and left little for the people who lived along shore. Instead of explorers, the boats brought tourists. Marvin told me that when he met them in town, they often didn't seem to know where they were.

Aside from the ships, Marvin said that most people he knew talked about change in terms of ice and animals. The great losses of summer sea ice were not really visible from Gjoa Haven, but in springtime the ice nearer to the mainland was becoming less predictable, more danger- ous to drive over. Long-established routes between distant communities seemed to be shifting, and things appeared even riskier on the ice that formed over freshwater lakes in the island's interior. There was one other phenomenon that Marvin said almost everyone agreed on: More wolves and polar bears were showing up on the tundra outside town, the *amaqqut* and the enormous *nanuit*.

"They didn't used to be here very much," Marvin said. "Like, when I was a kid, you didn't see them. Now they're here."

I asked where they came from and he waved a hand at the frozen sea, which opened below us to the south. It was afternoon. A golden glow washed over the ice, offering an illusion of warmth. I could not tell where land ended and sea began, and suddenly the rest of the world seemed very far away. I understood from Marvin's gesture that anything might be out there, anything at all.

MARVIN TURNED THE TRUCK AROUND AND DROVE TO a nearby garage where he wanted me to see something. Inside we found his snowmobile, which needed new axle bearings before the Ranger mission. We also met a young man named Paul, who worked as a federal conservation officer. The garage belonged to Paul's agency, and he'd let Marvin borrow the space out of sympathy: he knew how hard it could be to repair machines outdoors.

"I usually just do this kinda thing outside my house," Marvin said. "But in this kinda cold, your fingers end up hurting, eh? Touching all that metal."

Before he stuck his head into the machine he said to Paul, "Tell him about the bear."

Paul laughed and shook his head. The *nanuq* (the singular form of *nanuit*), he told me, was a female who'd started frequenting the town dump. Paul had managed to scare her off a couple of times with loud explosive shells that were like big firecrackers. But the bear kept coming back, and it wasn't long before the news had gotten around.

"People started driving out for a look at her," Paul said. "It was bad."

This was the sort of thing that got people mauled or killed. Paul and another man, named Adam, tried again to scare the bear off, and this time they circled her on their snowmobiles like cowboys, trying to drive her out to sea. It almost worked.

Paul walked over to a small freezer. He opened it, pulled out the bear's skull, and handed it to me. After she'd been shot, the bear had been skinned and butchered, and the meat distributed among elders in town. For them—though not for most younger people—bear meat was "country food," a delicacy from the old days.

I turned the skull over in my hands. It was enormous, still flecked with pink flesh. Under fluorescent lights the incisors gleamed. Once, twenty years before on Admiralty Inlet, I'd been chased over sea ice by a bear about this size. I escaped, but I knew I'd nearly become a parable. For a long time I had dreams about that bear. They were not exactly nightmares, more visions of color and motion—blue of ice, black of the bear's eyes, red vivid blood on his coat from a recent meal of seal. In the garage I pressed fingers to the dead bear's teeth, these scimitars of bone, and shuddered at the memory.

No one could say why the bear had come into town. I asked Paul if it was related to climate change and he demurred, the way people do when they sense you're testing a theory. I hadn't intended to do that and said so. Paul relaxed and guessed it was because the bear was young and not yet a very good hunter. He said bears were walking into northern towns more and more often, possibly because the ice had shifted up north, or seals were becoming harder to find.

It might also have been warming, he continued, which thinned and weakened the ice and made it less prone to forming the great miles-wide sheets the bears traveled over and used as hunting platforms. It might have been all of these things, or any of them. No one lived beyond Gjoa Haven, so there were few reliable ways to measure what was happening in the lives of animals further north. All Paul could say certainly was that the trend wasn't good for bears or humans.

"Killing a bear," he said, frowning. "It's just a pain in the ass." They were an internationally protected species. Such shootings—technically permitted, always second-guessed—tended to upset people down south. Paul sighed. "Lots of paperwork."

What remained now was the question of her hide and its lustrous fur. It was worth several hundred dollars. Should it go to Adam, the hunter whom Paul had asked to shoot her? Or could it somehow benefit the larger community, as the bear's meat had done?

Paul shrugged. A local committee would decide. Marvin, who'd been listening, suddenly stood and swiped grease from his cheek. He said everyone agreed the hide would make a great pair of pants.


WE EMERGED FROM THE GARAGE TO FIND THE DAY sliding toward twilight, though it was not very late in the afternoon. We drove around and ended up at the edge of town, out beyond the small airport and the cemetery, near the military radar that watched the skies for Russian jets or North Korean missiles. It was fully automated and also fully surveilled. You could walk up to it, Marvin said, and set off an alarm. Sometimes people did.

Marvin parked and we sat looking north over the land. After a few minutes he began to tell me that he'd once dreamed of leaving, of getting out of the Arctic. He told me he'd found a trade school in Ontario where he could learn to repair small engines, the kind that ran everything in the north, from snowmobiles and four-wheelers to generators and boat motors. He had planned to get certified or graduate and then come home to open a shop of his own.

At the time there was no such shop on King William Island. There were no such shops anywhere for at least three hundred miles. I understood that this was no mere daydream. Marvin had done what entrepreneurs are supposed to do. He'd identified a niche, envisioned a future.

"Genius," I said, and despite himself Marvin nodded.

"It was a good idea."

"What happened?"

Marvin brought the idea to his father and translated it into Inuktitut. Jacob listened carefully, patiently, and then he said no.

"He said, 'Your family is here. Why would you leave?'"

It wasn't much of a discussion. Marvin didn't appeal.

"We don't really go against our elders," he said.

There was more to the story, but I did not press. We sat and stared north. In that season the sky and the land were often the same gray-white and before us those two blank planes ran parallel all the way to the horizon where they fused along a sudden violet seam. It looked as though, way out there at the end of the world, someone was welding things together. Or prying them apart. The next morning we would head that way, on patrol.

Marvin reached for his mobile phone to check the time. "Oh shit," he said. "We gotta go."

He had to see a guy about ammo.

HAND OVER HAND, MARVIN AND I HAUL THE NET UP out of darkness. There's a slushy hiss as it emerges from the hole we've chopped through the ice. Our bare fingers burn with cold. The mesh feels like hot iron. Off to one side, Jacob watches, face hidden deep within his hood against the wind. We listen for his voice but the elder says nothing, so maybe that means we are doing it right.

It's late November, thirty below zero, night in the late afternoon. We stand on the frozen surface of Kakivaktorvik, the spear-fishing lake, hauling and peering down into the hole. In our headlamp beams we glimpse the first fish, a white form suspended in the gloom. There is an unexpected softness to it, a sensuality in the pale curve, like the arch of a woman's foot.

We pull. A trout appears. Another pull, another trout, then an Arctic char and a whitefish, then more trout. Each fish is some two feet long and we wrench the mesh from their gills and toss them writhing onto the snow. It is hard watching them die. Something about the way it comes, the air so much colder than the water, the light in their eyes fading, lenses crusting with ice. I don't know what kills them, cold or suffocation, but in their deaths I see our own. It would take so little. Just a crack in the ice, a snowmobile gone under. This is always my greatest fear in the north.

Water filling my boots and pulling me down. Everyone up here knows someone who's died that way. Every lake on the land has its resident ghosts.

I shake off the thought and toss another fish onto the snow. I am a guest and this was the work. Eventually we reset the net, guiding it back under the ice where it will hang in the black water like a nightmare. Then we wrap our catch in a blue tarp, climb onto our snowmobiles, and race east.

Marvin and Jacob are always faster. They beat me to camp by a quarter mile. When I catch up, they are stacking fish in a snowdrift outside our tent, the bodies already stiff, fins as brittle as old glass. Jacob lays some flat, the rest he jabs tailfirst into the drift, like fenceposts. Later, for breakfast, all we'll need to do is reach out the door and grab one.

When the little palisade of fish is complete, we duck into the tent and prepare for bed. We haven't taken many fish. All the other Rangers in camp have more. Their tents seem surrounded by fish, enough for weeks of eating. I asked Jacob about the difference, hoping to learn something about technique or experience or maybe luck. But he just shrugs. He starts humming a church song and gives me to know that the day and its work are done.

*Put your boots by the door.*

*A last cup of tea.*

*No more questions.*

WE HAVE BEEN OUT ON THE LAKE FOR A COUPLE OF days, and when I say *on* I mean atop: Our canvas tent sits on its frozen surface. Our floor is ice, and beneath our bed swim the fish we will eat. Later, when the floor starts to melt, we'll pack everything up and move. For now, all is solid beneath us and inside it is dim and quiet. The heavy cream-colored walls are streaked with grease, blood, mud, and frost. A patina of Arctic seasons.

Jacob and Marvin have set up a sleeping platform at the far end of the tent, and at night the three of us lie there shoulder to shoulder on an old foam mattress. Beneath it are spread several caribou skins. At the other end, beside the door, sits a Coleman double-burner. The stove is lit and for a week it will burn constantly, shut off only to change fuel canisters. Even when we are not cooking, even in the dead of night—which lasts much longer than the day—the low blue flame will be our companion, guttering away like an old friend, dancing in the draft that slips under the doors.

Sometimes I wake in the middle of the night to the sound of wind not blowing but heaving against the tent, shoving at it like some great beast, and I have no idea where I am. Then my eyes adjust. In the gaslight I see father and son sleeping beside me beneath piles of blankets. There is the floor, swept in snow. My backpack. A frying pan, a fish head. Jacob's piss can sitting there—an old coffee can that I must remember not to trip over. When I have accounted for all the things, like my toddler son back home, the blue flame whispers me back to sleep.

One thing I learn quickly out here is that when you are camped on the surface of a frozen lake, no one wants to talk about climate change. My plans, my questions, my desire to know about the transformation of the Arctic, all congeal like cold fat. So I discard them, mostly, and fall into the rhythm of our camp, where fifteen or so Rangers have set up half a dozen tents. Each day Marvin tries to do something martial; there have been a few training exercises, and every morning there is a meeting where the sergeant from the army talks about military things, about preparedness and "situational awareness."

The Inuit do not need to be reminded, though. The weather demands constant attention. For days we have hard wind and gray skies and temperatures hovering around thirty below. Down south we would call it an "Arctic blast," but those don't usually last like this. The cold keeps us close to camp. It conspires to make our world smaller. Life goes on, of course, but at a different pace and scale. I wonder how Jacob and his family lived during the igloo times. I learn to worry about the cold only when the Inuit retreat into their tents to smoke.

Our days revolve around the fishnets. Everyone checks them twice, once in the morning after tea and again in the evening before bed. It seems the men are always going out again to check and each time great shoals of fish give themselves up into air as sharp as glass. Day after day, night after night, so often that I start to wonder how many more could possibly live down there under the ice.

But the men keep pulling and the fish keep coming, as though hauled up from a well of desire. One evening I ask Marvin about it, thinking in southern terms of scarcity, of resources defined as renewable or nonrenewable, like trees or oil.

Marvin laughs at me and says, "We believe that as long as we share, they'll keep coming."

And my mind scratches, like a record, as the needle jumps a track.

THE DAYS SOON BLUR. THERE IS THE SUBTLE GRAY shift of snow over the surface of Kakivaktorvik, the way it drifts deep outside our doorway and begins to bury our fish. Once or twice we go out hunting caribou, but we are always driven back to camp by whiteouts. At night, Marvin and I lay in our sleeping bags, drinking hot fruit punch and talking about ghosts and white wolves. In the early mornings, Jacob always rises before us and begins making breakfast. In the gaslight I see his pajama pants with the little penguins on them. I look at my watch and though it says 5 a.m., out beyond the tent there is no hint of dawn. Only a darkness as deep as the sea.

Jacob often makes bannock in those hours, a fried bread that's a staple in Indigenous communities all over the north and down south, too. In other places it has other names and forms: sometimes it is fry bread or Eskimo donuts. Recipes change. Sometimes there is yeast, sometimes not. Often it is women who make it, though in Jacob's house Martha ceded the responsibility to him. On special mornings he adds raisins to the dough.

Breakfast, lunch, and dinner is fish. We occasionally eat them in soup but mostly raw. Jacob considers the eyeballs a delicacy: a pop of salt. Marvin prefers frozen cord blood, sliced thin, the taste of old coins. The lungs are wet cardboard. Everything else has a remarkable *untaste*, like the freshest sushi, like the water we drink from the lake.

One evening after Jacob is fast asleep, Marvin tells me that he's adopted. Inuit adoption isn't quite like the adoption practiced in the south. In Inuit culture, you might adopt a child whose parents couldn't support him, or whose parents had drinking problems. But a family might also give one of their children to another couple who had none of their own. You could also request a child, even one that had not yet been born. A Ranger named Adam, the one who shot the polar bear, told me how he and his wife had two children and then adopted out a third to some friends. A few years later, they wanted another baby and adopted one in from someone else.

None of this was unusual, jarring as it might sound to an outsider. The Canadian government recognized the practice. Official paperwork and signatures were required. Marvin and his partner, Ellen, had adopted their son, Marcus, a few years before I visited, when it became clear Ellen couldn't have children. Several years later, when I returned to see him, Marvin was about to adopt another boy. Jacob himself had been adopted many decades before. Marvin said even I could get adopted, if I really wanted to learn Inuit ways. He even had a prospective dad in mind for me—an old hunter named Paul Ikuallaq, the man who'd once thought he was related to Roald Amundsen. I could bother him with all my questions, Marvin said, and that made us both laugh for a long time.

I will come to understand the custom as rooted in a different concept of community, as well as in the unpredictability of hard winters and shifting sea ice. There was also sometimes a desire to pass on traditions. When I asked

Jacob about it later—about how it happened that he'd adopted Marvin when he was in his late forties and already
had adult children of his own—he gave a big smile, reached
out, and grabbed Marvin's arm. He said, in Inuktitut, "I
took him."

Marvin explained that his older brother, Jacob's natural
son, had health problems that prevented him from becoming a hunter. While he loved his son without reserve, this
was upsetting for Jacob, because he saw what was happening to his culture: the language loss, fewer people hunting,
the turn toward money, office jobs, the internet. He wanted
someone to whom he could pass his skills and his stories—
Utkuhiksalingmiut stories. Jacob approached a struggling
pregnant couple in town. Marvin told me that they, his
birth parents, would not have been able to support a child.
They agreed to give their baby to Jacob. Marvin still saw
his birth dad in town. Sometimes they hung out. But there
was never a question about who Marvin's *father* was.

ON SOME EVENINGS, AFTER THE DAY'S MILITARY EXERCISES
and after the fishnets have been pulled, Rangers go visiting.
This, too, is an old tradition, born of the polar night. Men—
and it was always men, for while there were women Rangers
in camp they tended not to take part—cram into someone's
tent and sit around drinking tea and telling stories. A few
times I accompany Marvin when he goes visiting, though
more often I stay behind. I know it's tiresome for him to
translate. I am fortunate, though, because Jacob, as the eldest Ranger, does less visiting. Instead, men come to him.

At those times, the stories turn first toward Jacob. He listens as others tell about the exploits of his life. He does not comment or add or correct. He merely sits there in his penguin pants, staring at the flame in the lantern, as though he is gathering up all the many versions of himself. Men tell of his hunting prowess, his generosity. The killer whale he caught, along with bears and caribou and musk oxen. And the seals, countless seals. A man named Saul, who is younger than Jacob but moves in the slow motion of a much older man, tells me that Jacob had been such a legend in his youth that he was afraid to speak to him. One day Saul and his brother were crossing the frozen sea by dogsled, heading south, when they ran into him. Jacob had staked out his dogs and was building an igloo for the night. He invited the younger men to overnight with him, and they could do little more than nod. That night Jacob made big rounds of bannock.

"He gave me a whole piece!" Saul says. His face shines with the memory. "And my brother, too. We had never had a whole piece of bannock like that. I couldn't eat it all. I had to put some of it away."

Other tales concern polar bears or mean dogs or the "starving times"—periods of famine that had spread over the mainland tundra and crushed Inuit communities as recently as the 1950s and '60s. One man, Simon, remembers that at some point after his family had eaten their dogs, a plane, a De Havilland Beaver, appeared flying low over the tundra. Through an open door a man shoved out miracles of flour, sugar, preserved meat.

When I research these starving times months later, their

clarity is stunning. The famines were linked to fluctuations in caribou migrations and the animals' failure to arrive at expected times, or in sufficient numbers. The Canadian government, so far away, always learned late of the dearth and was slow to help. More than anything else—more, say, than the allure of Western life, or schools or trade goods—it seemed famine was the force that ultimately swept Jacob's people, and perhaps all the remaining Arctic nomads, off the landscape and into towns like Gjoa Haven.

There in the tent, with wind howling around us over the black plane of the lake, these elders' lives seemed enormous. The smallest tale took on the dimensions and drama of the Arctic itself. In the years ahead, I would meet elders like these men in northern Alaska and hear similar tales. They all belonged to a last generation who'd known nomadic lives in North America long after most southern people assumed such cultures had gone extinct. A line had been drawn beneath their lives. It separated me from them, of course, but also the elders from Marvin or anyone younger. This was what people meant when they spoke of the igloo times. They were describing a vanished country, a way of being that had almost slipped out of reach.

The elders' mortality loomed. Here was the change the Inuit regarded with more concern than my proddings about a warming climate, or Amundsen, or the opening of the Northwest Passage and all the ships that slipped through it like the dreams of strangers. The Inuit were losing this generation even as they lost the ice. The cold was fading with memory.

After one evening full of stories Marvin tells me the

rest of his: Why he had decided to heed Jacob's plea and not go south to learn a trade. Why he had accepted command of the Rangers even though his brain had told him to refuse, to quit, to run.

"I know I don't have much time left with him. I want to make the most of it."

Marvin wants to learn everything he can. He wants, in other words, to be worthy. In the far corner of our tent the stove's blue flame mutters its approval.

ON OUR LAST MORNING AT KAKIVAKTORVIK, JACOB wakes me by singing happy birthday.

He dances in his penguin pajamas and croons the melody more than the words. He can't pronounce my name. He doubles over laughing and then Marvin and I laugh until we ache.

"It's your birthday?" Marvin asks, clutching his side.

"No."

We sip our tea and recover. Shadows flicker like water over the tent walls, steam from our mugs curls silver in the lantern light. I notice there are raisins in the bannock. Jacob begins telling us about his dream, and a thousand years of patience and survival seem to gather around us. In the dream, Jacob had been hunting caribou. They were so close. He knew he was dreaming and he did not want to wake.

Days later, on the long flight home, I find in a notebook the cramped details from an hour or two I spent alone with Jacob, before we traveled out onto the tundra. I was staying in a little rented house at the top of Gjoa Haven with the sergeant from the Canadian army, a guy named Dean. He and Marvin had gone out to run errands and Jacob stayed behind with me.

I made tea. We took our cups to the living room and sat on the floor. Outside a storm was moving over King William Island. Wind pushed snow as fine as dust under the front door, and every change in pressure made the whole house gasp and shiver. Jacob and I were silent, because we had no language in common. I was ashamed that I couldn't speak to him. Back then I believed that to honor him I needed to *inquire*, to ask questions.

After a while, Jacob reached into the pocket of his red Ranger hoodie and fished out a piece of string. He looped it between his massive fingers and soon the shapes of animals appeared, their bodies made of hoops and knots. Here was a running caribou, next a bouncing hare, then a wolf, a bear. A game as old as time. He deftly linked the animals, saying the name of each slowly in Inuktitut. *Tuktu, ukaliq, amaroq, nanuq.* As you would teach a child.

Beside him I watched, thrilled and suddenly afraid of the scale of all I did not know. In a few years, before I could return to see him, Jacob would die of complications linked to Covid-19. Now, he looked at me closely, saying nothing, fingers working.

Then he laughed and tossed me the rope.

# BARREN LANDS

*Hozi de / Northwest Territories*

FROM THIS SPOT ON THE BARREN LANDS, CARIBOU trails run off like railways over the emerald hills. The paths are innumerable, deep and straight, suggesting mass transit and common purpose—timetables, maps, an orderly procession toward expected ends. That is how it used to be, in the old days.

Hiking over the trails, it sometimes happens that you appear to step into the center of them, as though you're standing on the hub of a great wheel, gazing out over the spokes. In those moments it feels like you could pick any of the trails and walk it to the horizon. Maybe all the way north to the coastline, or back to the tree line, or even to the city of Yellowknife, 250 miles southwest. Looking out from the hub, you can see there is no place the caribou haven't been, no direction they haven't gone. The land isn't *barren*, it's busy with memories of caribou.

On a cool later summer day I choose a trail and follow, clumsily, slotting one boot in front of the other. Beside me, Roy Judas does the same. The animals' four-legged gait is narrower than ours, so we stumble. Even in huge herds they managed neat marches. I try to imagine the volume of animals required to shape the land this way, to impress their passage so firmly. Tens of thousands. Hundreds of thousands. Decades of migrations, the earth thrumming under their hooves.

"Used to be a highway for them," Roy says. "All gone now."

Roy is stout and athletic. He chews a stick, balances a Winchester lever-action across the beam of his shoulders. Today he is angry. Or, no, that's not quite right. I'm not sure there is a word for what Roy is. We've been looking for his caribou for days here in the far east of Canada's Northwest Territories, and we've seen only a handful. By *his caribou* I mean his people's, the Tłı̨chǫ, or Dogrib, a First Nation of the Dene. The caribou we seek belong to a herd called Bathurst, and there are so few left that even with the help of satellites and tracking collars and seasoned hunters like Roy, they have slipped away along these trails almost every time.

I thought it would be easier to find them. Caribou are big animals; adults weigh a few hundred pounds apiece. Once, not too long ago, there were half a million Bathurst caribou, and in certain places, during certain seasons, you could sit still and watch them stream past in a grand procession that might take days, or weeks. Now only about six thousand animals remain in the herd. That's still more Bathurst caribou than there are Tłı̨chǫ citizens, but in our time the landscape seems to swallow them. Almost as though it were reclaiming them, taking them back. This is one of Roy's fears. His herd is 98 percent gone. Perhaps the word for what he's feeling isn't anger, it's despair.

We trundle on, shunting tracks. Mosquitoes drone, Roy hums. He cusses. He buzzes. Keep moving, keep looking. He is not so much a restless man as one who, out here, is opposed to stillness. Stillness is sloth and sloth is laziness and laziness is losing the herd. Roy hates losing what he loves.

THE TŁĮCHǪ LIVE AT THE EDGE OF THE GREATEST wildlife mystery in North America. All across the top of the continent, caribou herds are declining, from Quebec in eastern Canada to the west coast of Alaska and beyond, into Russia. Those most affected are migratory tundra caribou, the great movers of the north. Annually they walk enormous loops between their winter feeding grounds, usually in or along the boreal forest, and their spring calving grounds on the Arctic tundra. Some herds—tracked by satellites—have been shown to travel farther than any other terrestrial mammal, nearly eight hundred miles in a year.

Migratory tundra caribou can be called many things across the vast spaces they inhabit: In Canada they are barren-ground caribou or eastern migratory caribou, while in Alaska "caribou" alone will usually do. In Russia and Norway, nearly identical animals are called wild reindeer. To the Inuit they are *tuktu*; to the Iñupiat, *tuttu*. The Tłįchǫ call them *ekwǫ̀*. Whatever their name, the species seems to be vanishing right before our eyes.

After an increase in numbers in the 1990s and early 2000s, caribou declined across their range by 65 percent, from about five-and-a-half million to less than two million. The National Oceanic and Atmospheric Administration, in its 2024 Arctic Report Card, shows that of about thirteen major herds in Canada, Alaska, and Russia, most have suffered steady losses. The Bathurst have fallen farthest. Several scientists lamented to me that we may watch them go extinct—as a herd, as a body of animals with a shared history, a shared memory, perhaps even a shared culture—within the next few years.

Scientists discussing the Bathurst are often quick to point out that losing a herd isn't necessarily unusual. They aren't permanent fixtures of the landscape. Herds routinely grow, shrink, atomize. Sometimes they blink out. This is not a very satisfying assessment for the Tłįchǫ, however, who have been in relationship with the Bathurst for hundreds or thousands of years. For them the questions are not rooted in biology or ecology but existence: If such a fate could overtake a beloved companion, the *more-than-human beings*, what might become of the people who depend on them?

Early one August I traveled with a small group of Tłįchǫ citizens to the barren lands of the Northwest Territories, to the eastern border of their land. We went by floatplane from Yellowknife; there were no roads where we were headed. To stare out the window at the landscape below was to watch the last of the boreal forest fade and then seem to vanish underwater. Here rose swamps and ponds, enormous dark lakes and silver rivers that branched and ran like strands of mycelium. In all this wet stood islands and carpets of green low brush and mounds of glacial soil, though even these seemed inundated, and at times it was impossible for me to know where liquid ended and solid ground began. Across this space we would search for Bathurst caribou, working as part of a Tłı̨chǫ government monitoring program.

Our camp sat on a small peninsula that knuckled up from the southeastern shore of a seventy-mile-long lake that on maps is called Contwoyto, though this is not a Tłı̨chǫ word. They call it Koketi. At the far end of camp stood an outhouse and in the center was the solitary cabin where we cooked and ate meals. Along the perimeter were our tents, in a haphazard row, each one covered with blue tarp to keep out the fierce rain that sometimes seemed not to fall so much as blast horizontally across the face of the earth. At the shore there was a short dock, a white motorboat rocking beside it. On a pole flew the wind-torn flag of the Tłı̨chǫ Nation, which gave you to know how they see themselves: four tipis made of caribou skin set against a dark blue field.

Most of the camp was enclosed with an electrified fence, to keep out the Big Men, the massive, shuddering *ursids* that could not be named (more on that later). Some mornings we find their huge footprints in the sand beside the dock, which means they visited us while we slept, when we were most vulnerable, and then they walked away.

On our first evening at camp, a woman named Janet Rabesca suggests I make an offering. It's about nine o'clock and the sky is still bright. She stands outside the little cabin, smoking. Inside, Roy is frying up trout just pulled from the lake. He has battered their bright orange flesh in flour, hoisin sauce, and ginger ale and the sweet scent runs out through the open door and stirs into Janet's smoke.

"You can give anything," she says. "Some grass, some flowers."

She tells me there's a pouch of tobacco kept here just for this purpose. The point is not the object but the intent. To give before we take, for we are all always taking. I feel a little ashamed for not knowing what to do, but she is not interested in that. She pats me on the shoulder. *Come on.*

We walk down to the lakeshore, passing through the electric fence. Janet carries some leaves of Labrador tea, *gots'agoò lidì*, a fragrant plant found here and all over the Arctic, used sometimes to make a fragrant hot beverage. I palm some tobacco. Silently we sift our plants into the water. It is so clear the leaves seem to glide over an invisible plane, casting tiny shadows on the sand below.

Back at the cabin Janet says, "All the shamans, the people who understood this stuff, are gone." A spray of freckles on her face, strands of gray in her dark hair. "We didn't have a chance to learn from them. There might be some left, but they keep themselves secret."

She hopes that's true, that shamans are out there, holding on to what everyone else has forgotten. There is very little medicine left in the world, she says. Or at least not many people who know how to use it. She is speaking of Indigenous medicine, that which is both medicinal and magical, gifts of the earth for healing and protection and learning.

"Climate change and everything else," Janet says. "People are sick, the land is sick."

All these symptoms and nothing for the cause.

EACH MORNING BEGINS IN THE CABIN, WITH A BREAK-fast of pancakes and bacon or eggs or cereal. There's a woodstove near the door and it's always hot, for while the days sometimes grow warm, the mornings are always cold. We are far enough north that August is just a shoulder season tipping toward winter. The ice didn't even melt off Koketi until July. In some places on the tundra we'll find patches of snow holding out, hiding in pools of shadow.

On the long dining table there are laminated topo-graphical maps of the lake and surrounding terrain. After eating—or sometimes before—Joe Lazare Zoe leads us in prayer. He holds a black rosary, but I don't hear a lot of Ca-tholicism in what he says. He invokes animals, ancestors, the Lord, the land. A specific application to our circum-stances. Joe is seventy-nine and an elder of the Tłıchǫ Na-tion. He has been to Koketi many times, even as a young man, back when to travel here meant walking and canoeing or hauling along a small folding boat, its little motor bal-anced over your shoulder like a rifle. In those days it took a long time to reach Koketi.

We look at the maps. Every few days, Roy gets a new set of satellite coordinates from the office back home. These correspond to Bathurst caribou who have been fitted with tracking collars. He plots the data. Some wolves are col-lared, too, and occasionally he plots their positions. Wolves are a little suspect out here. Many people think they're a malign force driving the decline not only of the Bathurst but of all tundra caribou, and in the Northwest Territories you might say wolves are less tracked than they are *surveilled*. Sometimes the government shoots them from helicopters, often hunters trap them or poison them. Down here wolves have learned the hard way to avoid us, though after Joe's prayer I make a small secret one of my own, hoping to see some.

Because the satellite coordinates are not fresh, Joe and Roy huddle and consider where the animals might have gone since they were last seen. The men factor in such variables as wind, rain, and sunshine, along with the presence of wolves. Normally mosquitoes would be a factor, too. Their harassment can significantly impact where and when a herd moves. In a bad year, the caribou spend a lot of the summer simply trying to escape plagues of mosquitoes. But this year has been cold, and I'm told the bugs aren't as bad as they could be.

Joe and Roy also take another dimension into their figuring: the accumulated experience of generations of Tłıchǫ hunters. This is not an assessment of data so much as it is a consultation with memory, with the past—with old stories and observations concerning where caribou have been found in previous years and decades. About this, Joe knows the most. In many ways he will come to remind me of Jacob Atqittuq in Gjoa Haven. Both men were about the same age, and both had come from another world. The Tłıchǫ didn't call it the igloo times, for they are people of the trees and did not build igloos. But Joe, I was told, is one of the few elders who both knows the old ways and still lives by them.

Roy, for his part, is thirty years younger and will readily admit he does not know the land and its stories as well as Joe. Roy minds Joe, defers to his experience. When they've mulled it over, analyzed all they can, the men pick a spot on the map to search for the Bathurst. Then the rest of us pack bags, fill thermoses, and climb into the fast white boat.

ROY ALWAYS DRIVES. HE SETTLES IN THE SEAT IN FRONT of the engine, chewing his stick, with his cap cinched tight so it can't blow off. This is his job, and he loves it: cold air washing over his face, the wide world of water open before him. On calm bright days Koketi is absolutely still, a mirror of the universe, and we fly between earth and sky. During these times, Roy lifts out of despair. He doesn't seem to feel the cold or the knives of the wind. But the rest of us do. We huddle along the bench seats, sometimes hide under a tarp. We are merely passengers then, witnesses to the joy of Roy.

No one knows why the caribou are disappearing. There's no consensus on what's behind this great vanishing. No disease has been pinpointed, no individual culprit gets the blame. Wolves were a popular villain mentioned nearly everywhere I went. Some people, almost always white, believed Indigenous hunters were killing too many animals. And in the Indigenous communities that make up nearly half of the Northwest Territory's population—and that stand to be most affected by caribou loss—mining was often seen as the greatest threat to the herds.

For people of a certain age, Joe's for instance, it was impossible not to notice that around the time the Bathurst seemed healthiest, in the 1980s and '90s, a handful of mines opened in the Northwest Territories and in the region that would become Nunavut. These included the gold mines Colomac and Lupin and diamond mines called Diavik and Ekati. All of them sprawled across the home range of the Bathurst, and the Lupin mine lay on the eastern shore of Koketi.

Caribou are members of the family *Cervidae*, related to white-tailed deer, elk, and moose. Beyond their ability to make enormous migrations, they are specifically well-adapted to the tundra, where they graze on both plants and lichens. The lichens are what sustain caribou through winter and early spring, and they use their spade-like hooves to find patches of them beneath the snow. Like other *Cervidae*, caribou are generally skittish around humans and sensitive to disturbances in their environment. With the mines came plenty of both. Roads, helicopters, low-flying planes, construction noise. Clouds of dust blew up wherever the ground cover was torn away and it later settled over the tundra, coating caribou forage.

Two of the mines, Diavik and Ekati, were on Tłı̨chǫ land, and this complicated things. Jobs and mine money poured into the Nation. The Northwest Territories reaped hundreds of millions of dollars from the mines. In the last decade, federal and territorial governments have been more willing to incorporate Indigenous traditional knowledge into the planning and operation of mines, though there is so much money involved, and extraction seems so certain to continue and even expand, that many of the Tłįchǫ I spoke with were not optimistic. They believed that if it became a choice between caribou and minerals, the territorial government would choose the latter.

Another potential cause of caribou decline was, of course, climate change. Warming is heavily implicated in the great vanishing, and changes to caribou habitat can already be measured in several ways. The North American Arctic and sub-Arctic are generally becoming greener, thicker with plant life—a process often called "shrubification." In some places new kinds of plants are appearing, too, species that have crept north as summer temperatures rise and growing seasons lengthen. While it isn't clear that new plants are replacing caribou forage—turning the tundra into a salad caribou won't eat, as one expert put it—several researchers said that shifting vegetation could affect herds' health, or even their migration patterns. Winters have also grown wetter in some parts of the far north. This becomes a problem for caribou when rain or wet snow falls and then freezes, locking crucial lichens away under lids of impenetrable ice.

Still, the term climate change has become less a diagnosis than a kind of collective sigh. The term is shorthand for forces so entangled they appear like a thread with a million fibers. It isn't yet possible to tease apart every cause and consequence and decide how it might be affecting caribou. And while there are straightforward ways to reduce warming—cutting fossil fuel use, for example—

none has ever been seriously considered by any North American government. Instead, governments have taken half measures. They've shot wolves and bears and called it predator management. Or they've regulated hunting, which mostly affects Indigenous communities. In Canada and the U.S., both approaches have been tried, but neither has stopped or even seemed to slow the decline.

To anyone who lives far south of the Arctic Circle (and that is most of humanity), the problem, when it is seen at all, can appear abstract, another distant note of sadness in an era heavy with extinctions. That's not how it looks up here. In small communities scattered below the tree line or set in the open tundra, towns like Wekweètì, where Roy grew up, or many others I would visit, the problem is existential. These towns are often isolated, often Indigenous, where imported food and gas can be astronomically expensive and hunting caribou is often the cheapest and fastest and certainly the most satisfying way to provide for a family. Here the decline brings a peculiar dread.

In a coastal Alaskan town a few years after my visit to the Tłıchǫ, an Iñupiaq elder would tell me that watching caribou disappear was like feeling a cold coming on. The cold settles in. It lays hold of your body and it lingers. You don't get over it. Then it worsens, until you become gaunt and haunted, until you're afraid it isn't a cold at all but something deeper. Something shot through your whole system.

Out on Koketi, the Tłıchǫ didn't seem willing, or perhaps interested, in trying to blame any one cause. By then I had learned not to ask about such things too directly or too often, and so I don't press anyone. Once, while cruising past the now-shuttered Lupin mine, I ask Roy what he believed was behind the vanishing. It's late afternoon. Koketi is flat and calm. Roy slows the boat slightly but says nothing. He merely turns toward Lupin and lifts his chin.

IN 2010 THE GOVERNMENT OF THE NORTHWEST TERritories set a partial hunting ban over the Bathurst herd. By 2015 a total ban was in place, and though the Tłı̨chǫ government supported the ban, many of its citizens were unhappy. They knew what it meant: The most significant activity through which they bonded with the herd would be closed off. Hunting isn't merely hunting to the Tłı̨chǫ or any other Indigenous group I've spent time with. The better term now is harvesting, and in its plainest manifestation this involves stalking, catching, and killing an animal, gathering meat and hide, bones and organs. This is intensely physical work, but it's inseparable from spiritual practice, too. Hunting is often understood as the fulfillment of a relationship. Among the Tłı̨chǫ, hunting was a human role, even a duty. The caribou had a complementary one, and that was to give themselves to worthy people, just as whales did in the Iñupiaq story I'd heard long before.

Here appears the messy edge of the contract, though, of the bond between animal and human. To some ways of thinking, and in some old stories, if humans do not fulfill their obligations, the caribou may decide to leave—walk right off this plane of existence. I met Tłı̨chǫ who believed this could happen. One of them was Tammy Steinwand-

Deschambeault, director of the Department of Culture and Lands Protection for the Tłı̨chǫ government.

"If we're not on the land, the caribou think that they're not needed," she told me one day, after I had returned from Koketi and visited the Tłı̨chǫ town of Behchokǫ̀. "They might decide to go away. So we need to go back to being out on the land more, you know—attend to these kinds of relationships. We have to do our part."

Modern life, town life, a hunting ban—all these things conspired to keep people and caribou apart. After the ban, the Tłı̨chǫ created Ekwǫ̀ Nàxoèhde K'è, a program to send their citizens out onto the tundra, to the leading edge of the mystery. The name means, roughly, "following in the trails of the caribou." In English it's also called Boots on the Ground. Each summer, small groups of citizens do what Roy and Joe and Janet and the rest of us were doing: They travel to Koketi to search for caribou. Not to hunt them, of course, but to observe. To record what they're up to, where they're headed, what they are eating, who's eating them. Observers also watch for climate indicators, such as increasing vegetation or unusual species of plants. This data is then used to help inform the Nation's hunting policies and management decisions.

To the extent that a herd of migratory animals can be managed across a range almost half as large as the Northwest Territories itself, it's done collaboratively: by the Tłı̨chǫ, the territorial government, and more than a dozen other Indigenous groups. In the early days of this arrangement, Steinwand-Deschambeault told me that the Tłı̨chǫ had been dependent on the government for data on the Bathurst. At that point the herd had shrunk to such a degree that it was difficult to find them, see them. The Tłıchǫ Nation didn't have the resources to collar caribou and track them with satellites or fly aerial surveys of the herd. They didn't have the training to analyze blood, genetics, or toxicology.

What they *could* do was invite people to Koketi. Ask them to live on the land and follow the Bathurst.

"The main reason for creating the Boots on the Ground program was for our own Tłıchǫ people to be the eyes and ears of what's happening out there with the caribou," Steinwand-Deschambeault said. "The elders didn't want to rely on the territorial government or anybody else to say, 'This is what's happening, this is what we're seeing.' The elders said, 'We need to see for ourselves.'"


JOE WAS ONE OF THOSE ELDERS. HE WAS TALL AND SLIM, with a bristle mustache and patient way of speaking. He always wore a camouflage baseball cap. Once he compared me to a priest because I took so many notes. I am not certain it was an insult, though he added that when he was a child it was the priests who taught him how to cuss. In town, he said, they always cussed when they kicked stray dogs.

In the Tłıchǫ language, Koketi means "old camp lake," or, more roughly, "lots of camps by the water." For thousands of years people had been traveling there to hunt caribou. In the days before gasoline engines, getting here took weeks, months. You journeyed through that landscape of water, a labyrinth of lakes, rivers, and marshes, over sodden tundra that quivered underfoot. Because they could not carry much on their shoulders or in their canoes, people arrived to Koketi hungry. Expectant.

That's how it was, Joe tells me one evening. He had just finished explaining that you could tell different herds of caribou apart by the taste of their flesh.

"Out here, people live with the animals. They're not gonna grow vegetables, nothing like that. Their food, their clothing, their life, comes from the animals."

We sit high on the esker behind camp, looking over the land. Nearby Janet has found a lithic scatter—the shards of waste left by a toolmaker, someone who sat in that place, turning a stone into a knife or an arrow point or a scraper. The small gray flakes lie where they fell, in a way that suggests the toolmaker sat facing north two hundred years ago, or four hundred, or a thousand. It's possible to imagine him looking out over the endless green plain, watching for the subtle shift in light that gives away caribou moving under the horizon. There are some out there, now, far away, but Joe says they're not Bathurst. You can tell by the color of their coats, which are bright, almost white when the light hits them. A few years earlier I'd learned that the Inuit used to call big caribou herds *the lice of the earth*, for the way they seemed, when observed from a distance, to crawl.

"Those old people were really tough," Joe says. He looks at the lithic scatter, then out at the land and the caribou, which appear impossibly distant, shimmering like a mirage. "You know how they did it? Really did it?"

"No."

"Medicine," he says. "They had powerful medicine."

What I understand is that the journey to Koketi was

not merely a gamble, not only a grueling physical slog toward some lake. You didn't come here on a whim, merely hoping to intersect with caribou. Instead, you made a pilgrimage. You kept the appointment.

Nearly every day, we walk through the places where the ancient people slept, waited, laughed. We hike through meadows bright with white cotton grass and through "forests" of dwarf birch that rise only a couple of inches from the ground. We follow the paths of the caribou and we find, during our wandering, that it seems humans have been everywhere, too. We find their lance points and arrowheads, we find half-buried hearths that still brim with charcoal and burned bone. In many campsites glacial cobbles still lie arranged in rings: These once held down caribou-skin tents. There are also hunting blinds built of boulders so large you wonder how humans ever moved them.

We also find more recent things in our walking. From a century ago we discover old bullet casings and rusted cast-iron pans. One day I find a whirligig, a kid's toy cobbled together of wood and slivers of tin from a tobacco can. And we find shards of plastic from our own era, abandoned oil drums, and perfectly smooth cylinders of stone. These are drill cores, extracted from below the permafrost by prospectors who came looking for gold, what the Tłįchǫ call "money rock."

SLOWLY THE OLD CAMPSITES AND ARTIFACTS BEGIN to haunt us. Not in the way of ghosts but for the abundance they speak of, the wealth we can no longer see.

Days in the boat, days spent hiking. We chase stale coordinates. All we manage to see is a solitary caribou there, or there. Most days Joe seems to have more caribou in his pocket, in a ziplock full of dried meat, than there are moving over the land. Other animals seem plentiful. One day Joe spots the largest herd of musk oxen I have ever seen, perhaps three dozen or more of them slowly mowing their way through the afternoon's hot haze. Another time a white wolf walks through our camp. She is young and bold, though not as bold as the wolves on the Fosheim Peninsula. She slips under the electric fence, which means one of us forgot to turn it on, and slides past the outhouse and our tents, keeping a steady eye on us. I feel as though I should speak to her. Ask if she has any news. Before I can, she shimmies under the fence at the far end of camp and is gone, sauntering a little, like a kid who's just won a dare.

Then there are the *ursids*. Among the first things I learned out here was to not call a bear a *bear*, and so I shall not anymore. The thinking went like this: on the tundra, everything has a name, every animal has language. And in this open country the wind can carry a word farther than the eye can see. Saying a name can sometimes summon the thing, and of all the animals, it is the massive barren ground grizzlies who, the Tłı̨chǫ believe, are most likely to hear their name and come looking for whoever spoke it. That's why they call a grizzly a Big Man.

"See it from his perspective," John Boline, the camp guard, had told me one evening. We were standing high on an esker behind camp, watching a Big Man root through a distant patch of willows. He was digging ground squirrels out of their burrows with an almost playful rhythm. *Dig, pounce, chomp; dig, pounce, chomp.* John stood at my shoulder, cradling an old Winchester rifle wrapped in a dirty white cloth.

"Imagine you're a Big Man. You're out there, minding your business, looking for food, and then you hear your name. 'Bear! Bear!' Well, of course you're gonna look up and go have a see."

Down in the willows the young Big Man was resplendent, his coat as rich as chocolate. When the light shifted he seemed dipped in silver. We couldn't stop staring, and so it felt like a loss when he dropped out of sight. But he soon reappeared, lurching up from behind a nearby knob of earth. He was climbing the esker, head high, nose in the wind. Coming up toward us.

"Holy shit," Janet whispered.

Joe picked up two large stones and rapped them together, a jarring *clack* that rattled my teeth. Janet pressed a bear banger, a small explosive charge, into my hands and then retreated. John slipped the cotton sleeve off his rifle. He began to shout in Tłįchǫ.

"We're not here for you, Big Man! Go away!"

The Big Man ignored him. Shoulders rolling, nose black and working. With each step a thick layer of fat rippled beneath his fur. This was a confident animal, aware of his size and primacy. For a moment I wanted it both ways. I wanted him closer; I wanted all of us safe.

"Go away, Big Man!"

John pulled out his own bear banger and fired. Pop of smoke, a tiny trail of light. Then a *bang*, which was swallowed instantly by the wind. And yet somehow it worked. The Big Man turned and jogged away, all that fat shivering like Jell-O, the light splashing off him in sheets.

"He's young," said Joe. "He don't know people yet."

"I hope he don't come," John said. "Don't want to shoot him."

"Screw this!" said Janet from somewhere behind us.

But still she hovered, caught there in a kind of superposition, terrified and awed, her slight frame tense and ready to run.

During the next half hour, we saw two more Big Men. One was truly gigantic. He plowed through the brush and the willows, his shoulder hump parting the sea of leaves like a shark's fin. But he and the other Big Man were intent on their feeding and didn't bother to look at us. We watched them for a while, accepting the gift of their presence, until the cold forced us home.

Later, in the cabin, we came down from the encounter over cups of weak tea. A log popped in the woodstove. A living quilt of mosquitoes settled over the window screen.

John worried that the first Big Man, the young one, wasn't finished with us. Joe agreed that he'd probably come creeping around camp. I stared down into my notebook, stuck on language.

"What do you call a female?" I asked. "Big Woman?"

John snorted his tea.

Janet scowled.

Joe just said, "No."

Later John walked down to the electric fence and checked to see it was on.

THE BARREN LANDS WERE PROBABLY GIVEN THEIR name by a miserable British explorer.

Samuel Hearne, the explorer who was also an employee of the Hudson's Bay Company, is one suspect. He struggled through Tłı̨chǫ territory and went north onto the tundra in the late 1700s, searching in vain for deposits of copper. White travelers from that time rarely returned with positive reviews of the landscape that lay between the trees and the Arctic. The very things they came here to do—measure, map, fill in blank spaces, and drag unknown places into British or French comprehension—were maddeningly difficult. The landscape resisted their desires. For men whose minds had been shaped in Europe on much tamer terrain, the tundra looked empty and bleak. Almost perversely useless. None of the crops they valued would grow here. None of the animals they husbanded could survive here. And the notions they carried—their measures of wealth and meaning, their senses of faith and property and government—seemed wholly unfitted to the place.

The Tłı̨chǫ conceived of the land, and of space itself, very differently. In their understanding of creation, every *where* was inhabited. There was no such thing as emptiness, no place the creator had somehow forgotten to populate. Instead, a place might be home to beings that simply couldn't be seen by ordinary means.

The Tłı̨chǫ divide the barren lands into two parts: *hozi*, which was nearer to the tree line, and *hozi de*, which was closer to the Arctic coast. A Canadian archaeologist named Tom Andrews once told me that *hozi de*, where I traveled with the Tłı̨chǫ, was a term concerned with winter. There was also the sense that in *hozi de* you might encounter the Inuvialuit, an Inuit people who lived in the western Arctic but who often came far enough south that a Tłįchǫ hunter could encounter them. Caution was implied. The two peoples weren't always friendly.

Those old tensions were gone, but the concept of inbetweenness lingered in some ways. *Hozi* and *hozi de* implied a transitional space that separated the cultures, languages, and ecosystems of the forests and those of the Arctic coast. Such spaces were everywhere in the north, for there were rarely any hard edges.

It had even been possible in the old days, before the missionaries crushed such beliefs, for Tłįchǫ hunters to transition into caribou—to *become* them, and then later return to human form. Some Iñupiat, in Alaska, believed the same. Becoming caribou was a way to learn from the animals, to see the land as they did. It made you a better, more conscientious hunter. Modern borders, perhaps like many modern identities, were opposed to such fluidity. They were sudden, often militant statements that offered no room for transitions. They demanded that you pick a side, pledge allegiance. They were a colonial imposition, perhaps best applied to the movements of white people.

DRAWN ACROSS THE MIDDLE GROUNDS OF THE FAR north, stitching *hozi* and *hozi de* together with their lives, are migratory tundra caribou. The Bathurst is only one of about half a dozen herds moving over the barren lands, and during their annual journeys these animals cross every kind of natural border, walking from forests onto taiga and into tundra, passing through swamps, over rivers, and across lakes. Their hooves pull up the earth and their droppings fertilize it, along with their placentas, their stillborn calves, and of course their corpses. In death they become food not only for humans or wolves, but for entire ecosystems, including bears, eagles, foxes, and wolverines. Rodents gnaw on their bones and antlers. Lichen and algae eventually colonize whatever remains.

Over several years spent studying caribou, I have sometimes found it useful to think of them as similar to salmon, with caribou migrations resembling the great fish runs that occur each autumn along the west coast of North America. When I've mentioned this to scientists, they often balk—the spawning runs of Chinook, Chum, and Coho, the fish I'm thinking of, are so massive in terms of biomass that it's difficult to compare them to anything. But when you loosen the focus on numbers and consider other aspects of the animals' journeys, you begin to see how fish and caribou feed entire landscapes. How they push into remote corners of the continent bringing nutrients and energy. When you hold their two kinds together in your mind, you begin to sense forces at work that are, for now, far beyond scientific understanding.

Both caribou and salmon are drawn to specific geographic locations that are imprinted on them at the very beginning of their lives. In the case of caribou, each herd is drawn to a unique calving ground on the tundra: the areas where they were born. Salmon, of course, return to the rivers in which they were conceived, where they hatched, and where they lived as alevins and fry. While salmon return to their home streams only once, to reproduce and die, caribou make the trip every spring. Pull back a few degrees from these differences and what becomes most obvious is the cyclical nature of their journeys. Over and over and over their kinds have come, salmon bodies creating rivers within rivers, building into floods of flesh and bone, while caribou herds flow more like tides, surging from the trees to the tundra and draining back again.

Salmon and caribou belong to a group of animal movers that also shaped human life and helped it flourish in the time before colonization. Other animals in this group include bison, geese, seals, walrus, and whales—all migratory beings with whom humans kept appointments, and for whom they crossed plains, mountains, and even the frozen sea. After colonization, hard lines and borders began to disrupt those movements. Roads, dams, and pipelines; fences, railways, and clear-cuts of old growth. These made it impossible for many of the migrators to fulfill their destinies or to distribute their gifts. For now, migratory tundra caribou remain one of the few species left that still complete their ancient role, across much of their ancient range.

Only by searching for them, by walking the land with the Tłįchǫ, was I able to glimpse how the herds, in their way, held everything together. How they provided not merely for one tribe or one species of carnivore, but all of them. Somewhere out on the barren grounds I realize I have only been thinking of the people—of what will happen to them if caribou herds crumble. Suddenly I am overwhelmed with worry for the land itself.

I WANT TO TELL YOU THAT WE FOUND CARIBOU. FOR two weeks we search, cruising up and down Koketi, roaming the lonely tundra along its shores. Our bad luck seems to weigh heavily on Roy. He had learned to hunt when the Bathurst were at their peak, in the 1990s. He became a man just as their numbers began to crash. He knows he is watching a world pass away.

One day we are on the eastern side of Koketi, hiking along a great green slope that's fuzzed with mosses and dwarf birch and broad patches of pink cloudberry. The land rises gently eastward. Roy and I are waiting for the others in our little group. I am lying face down in moss, listening to mosquitoes whine around my ears. I breathe in damp scents of flint and something that smells of pine, or eucalyptus. I lift my head, focus on what spreads directly below my nose: Labrador tea, cup lichen, sphagnum moss, and many others I do not know.

The mat of vegetation is dense, enjambed as verse and colorful as a Persian rug. It's a few inches thick, swirling with emerald and crimson, copper and gold. I sink my fingers in and work them down until I feel the cold hard soil below. Also here are blueberries and cranberries. Now and then I reach out to pick a few. When I pull my hand back it is gray with mosquitoes.

Nearby Roy sits on a boulder with his rifle in his lap.

"What da fuck," he says to himself. "DA FUCK?"

He's impatient with the others. They're up on a ridge, scanning the empty country farther east.

We have come to the far edge of Bathurst territory. We are more firmly now in the home range of a herd called

Beverly. The Beverly are also declining, though not nearly so badly as the Bathurst. In 2018, a few years before my journey to the barren lands, a survey found slightly more than a hundred thousand caribou in the herd. Not great and not dire, holding a middle ground against the tide.

Roy tells me that the Tłıchǫ had recently observed Beverly animals entering Bathurst territory, coming farther west than anyone alive could remember. While I push my face deeper into the moss he says the Beverly were poking around like prospectors, trying out new pastures, maybe so they could move in when the Bathurst went *poof*. He was joking. But he also worried it might be true.

Roy was forty-seven that summer. Divorced. His only son lived far to the south. Back in his hometown, Wekweètì, he belonged to a family of chiefs and politicians, though he aspired to be neither. What he really wants to do, he says, is to "find some fucking caribou."

His voice goes suddenly harsh. I pull my face out of the moss and roll over.

He grins to let me know he's okay, then he holds his arms wide, taking in the absolute stillness around us, the old caribou trails etched into the earth at our feet. *Da fuck?* I see him then, for a moment. The weight of his worry, the fear below the jokes. He'd reached an age where loss tried to settle in, like a kind of weather. Emptiness was eating at him even as it spread over the landscape.

In the winters Roy worked for the territorial government, monitoring the Bathurst herd and helping to enforce the hunting ban. It didn't always make him popular with his neighbors. Once he'd even caught an old friend hunting the caribou. Roy didn't care. He hadn't taken the job for *people*. Slowly, though, people seemed to be coming around to his way of seeing things.

"What way is that?"

Roy spits loudly. "I want there to be caribou in the future."

A TERRITORIAL BIOLOGIST NAMED JAN ADAMCZEWSKI had told me that in recent winters the Bathurst had been mixing with the Beverly. I didn't bring it up with Roy that day; he wasn't in the mood. But I was thinking about it, and I do still. Adamczewski said the Bathurst caribou might have been seeking safety in the Beverly's numbers. Maybe they would eventually fold themselves into the larger herd. It might be possible for them to recover that way, he said, by which he meant *to survive*.

If they did, if they joined another herd, the Bathurst's singular culture would probably collapse. They would not migrate the same way, they would not graze the same plains or return to the same calving grounds year after year. Maybe even the taste of their flesh would change.

"If we lose one of these herds, there's a lot in terms of behavioral memory that we also lose," Adamczewski said. "When caribou don't visit their traditional calving grounds, they don't seem to live as long."

Seen against other changes unfolding in the far north, including the greening tundra, melting sea ice, and burning forests, the unraveling of the Bathurst appeared almost like a symptom of dementia. Like the landscape forgetting itself and its stories.

In some ways the Tłįchǫ fear the same things. If you are a caribou people and your caribou disappear, what do you become? I have no way to answer this question. I know only that the Tłįchǫ are well aware of it, and they are not the only northern people asking.

Looking north from my home in New York City, the closest wild migratory tundra caribou roam some thousand miles away, in Ontario. Even for me, after years spent thinking about them and traveling across their ranges, the animals are often out of sight, out of mind. Less like a fellow being and more a distant idea, a shadow drifting over the map. Multiply this conceptual distance across most of our lives, and you see why their fate doesn't summon a sense of alarm in the capitals of Ottawa or Washington.

A few years ago, I hung a caribou antler up in my apartment. It'd been given to me by an Alaskan hunter, and I placed it conspicuously, hoping my sons might show interest. For a week, they did, but I realized quickly there was nothing deeper in which I could ground their attention, not in the city. Down here we have no relationships with animals that even approach the complexity of the Tłįchǫ's with caribou. We are so removed from such things that we have trouble recognizing them, or bestowing validity upon them. Most people who visit my apartment never guess what kind of animal the antler comes from. They just want to know if I killed it myself.

"POW!"

When we finally find the Bathurst, Roy is so pleased he pretends to shoot them.

"Pow!"

Roy fires off another imaginary round, aiming this time at a big, beautiful cow. She raises her head. In the shimmer you can see flies dancing between her antlers. She searches for the sound and when she spots us, she lifts her nose, as though in disgust, and trots off. She is followed by a tiny brown blur—a calf, barely two months old, that had been hidden behind a rock.

Roy puts down his rifle. He grins and watches mother and calf go. They wander away through the high, rock-lined meadow, heading vaguely south and following a well-worn trail. Joe says something in Tłįchǫ and both men laugh.

We had to cross into the Arctic to find them. We had taken the boat for hours to the northern end of Koketi, then hiked up beyond the Arctic Circle. We were nearer than ever to the Bathurst's calving grounds, deep into *hozi de*, and at first the landscape had been empty. We had almost given up, almost turned around, and then they came to us. Someone shouted *There!* and soon a wave of animals was approaching, grazing slowly over the plain. The day was almost hot. The caribou took their time. I had never seen the Tłįchǫ happier.

"They look good," Joe says. "They look fat."

It was his highest compliment.

We sit and watch the animals for an hour. It's a small herd, maybe twenty or thirty mothers and calves and yearlings, but they are enough. For a while we can almost forget they are vanishing, that they are maybe forgetting who they are.

"Caribou and people, they always like to see each

other," Joe once told me. "They like to be around each other. When something bad happens in someone's life, if their husband dies or their wife, someone gets sick, they want to go where the caribou are. Then they feel better."

It was the old relationship, one that defied reason in the southern mind, in the rational duality of predators and prey. Here instead were fellow citizens, traveling through time, over the land, together. I thought of the trails cut deep into the earth and how many of them Joe had followed. The caribou had once made the barren lands feel full. They came down from the north bringing heat and gifts. Maybe healing, too.

"They make things less lonely," Joe had said.

The herd begins to drift away. Joe stands and raises his arms wide over his head, fingers splayed. It's a hunter's trick. He is making himself look like a caribou, turning his arms into a big rack of antlers silhouetted against the sky. He's done this many times before. The caribou almost always stop and raise their heads and sometimes they step nearer. But Joe is not trying to trick them. What he wants is for them to stay. What it looks like now is prayer.

Roy and Janet and I wonder if it will work. The caribou are close enough that we can hear the peculiar click of their hooves, a sound like castanets. Their wet wool scent fills the air. All we desire is to look, maybe talk with them a little. Maybe if we look hard enough or long enough or speak with enough love then the last of them won't leave.

# LAST OF THE NOMADS

*Anaktuvuk Pass, Alaska*

STAND ALONE IN A CLASSROOM NEAR THE TOP OF Alaska listening to the tick of a clock. Books sag in their shelves along the wall, and an American flag hangs limp over a window. Cold pale light pours in from an early spring day. On the floor before me is a young female caribou. She is dead, shot an hour or so ago on the tundra. The teenage boys who killed her out in the valley brought her to the school on a green plastic sled and then more boys, from the volleyball team—they'd been practicing in the gym—helped carry her body inside. The lift left puddles of blood and ice gleaming down the hall.

In the classroom, desks were pushed aside and a bed of cardboard was arranged on the floor in preparation for a different kind of education. The caribou was laid on top. She was a few years old and not very big. Her antlers were

thin and her feet, when I lifted them for a look at her magnificent, spade-like hooves, were no larger than my hand.
A bright gash ran down her belly: The boys gutted her out
there, on the land, and left the stomach and intestines for
the wolves. The rest, all of her organs, they have kept intact.
When I ask a teacher if the body will spoil or start to stink
as it lies here overnight, she assures me it won't be a problem. "That hair will keep her insulated. Good and fresh."

In the morning, the whole student body, from high
schoolers to first graders, will gather around the caribou
and, under the careful instruction of an eighty-one-year-
old elder, they will skin and then butcher it. They will
learn the proper names for organs and limbs in their native
language, all the muscles and joints, too. They will practice using knives the way their grandparents did, with an
eye toward economy, spare movements meant to make the
most of every part. The meat will be cut up into chunks,
slipped glistening into ziplock bags, and later, distributed
among local families who need it, families who, for one
reason or another, can't hunt for themselves.

During the workshop there will be a lot of laughter.
The kids' hands will get slick with blood. It will smear
their faces. They will enjoy themselves immensely. There
will also be a reverence for the work, and for the caribou
herself. Nothing loud or fancy, just a quiet sort of thanks.
Every kid in the classroom has grown up eating caribou.
Every kid knows where they come from and how they are
caught, and they know death is part of the deal. Almost
every one of them considers *tuttu* to be their favorite meal.

At some point during this workshop, the elder leading

it will have a heart attack. He won't recognize it as that, none of us will, and so he merely sits down, feeling a little winded. The kids, the teachers, the old man's daughter—no one has any idea how soon they will lose him, one of the few people left who remembers the old ways. He smiles through the whole thing, then sits, telling a few stories about what life was like when he was their age, when their people still lived as nomads, following caribou through the mountains. It was not that long ago, after all.

But these things will come tomorrow. For now I am alone, listening to the clock, standing over the body. I kneel and put my hands on the caribou's coat and push my fingers down deep, to her skin, where she is still warm. They are not like the wolves of Ellesmere. Caribou do not ever let humans near. I am briefly saddened to realize I will probably get no closer to them than this, after they are dead and before they are food.

Out in the hallway a teen, who was one of the hunters, is wiping up blood. His name is William. He tells me that when he's done, he wants to go back out and keep hunting. If it were up to him, he would hunt all day, every day, and especially now, during *upingnagskraq*, spring.

"They're coming," he says. At this point he is not so much cleaning as painting, pushing the blood around in absent-minded arcs with a saturated paper towel. He's just distracted, gone giddy on caribou.

"Every day there are more," he says. "The hills are full of them."

He looks up. In his bright smile there is joy, love, pride— happiness. Then he ducks back down to the blood work.

BY THEN I'D BEEN IN TOWN FOR A COUPLE OF WEEKS. There were caribou in the hills when I arrived, in late March, and they kept coming. I saw them every day. Sometimes you could even smell them, with the right kind of easterly, their sweet earthiness drifting down the snow-covered streets like the scent of some early blossom. Soon the better part of the Western Arctic herd, nearly two hundred thousand animals, would flow through this valley and adjacent ones. Soon animals might outnumber humans here by nearly five hundred to one.

I'd come for that, for abundance. For almost a year, biologists and anthropologists had been telling me that to truly see the other end of the line, a place where the human-caribou relationship was not so marked by loss, I should visit the Nunamiut, in Anaktuvuk Pass. They lived a thousand miles west of the Tłı̨chǫ and were even more isolated. There were no settlements of any size within 150 miles of Anaktuvuk Pass, and the town was also surrounded by Gates of the Arctic National Park and Preserve—8.5 million acres of almost completely uninhabited wildland. This vast space seemed to act as a shield for caribou, offer some kind of defense against the decline of their kind, though no one could say if it was real or would last. What was clear was that the Western Arctic herd had not yet been devastated.

It wasn't that the animals were immune. Their numbers were falling and would continue to fall. Long after I left Anaktuvuk Pass, I would watch them diminish from afar. At the time, though, in 2021, they were among the largest herds in North America. But tremors of worry ran through the community of scientists and wildlife managers who kept official watch over them, who saw what was happening to the Bathurst and feared it would hit the Western Arctic herd next. Most of them understood there existed a fine line between abundance—a natural kind of self-sustaining plenty—and mere good luck, in which things feel tenuous, vulnerable. This turn seemed already underway for the Western Arctic herd, and people wondered if their luck might finally be about to turn bad.

Still, there remained a kind of calm, an appreciation for the robustness of the Western Arctic herd. One biologist said he and his colleagues were in a holding pattern, a "wait-and-see mindset." He also admitted there was nothing else anyone could do. The Western Arctic herd caribou might be observed, counted, collared, and tracked, but like any animal studied under the lens of science, we could not really understand their whole selves, by which I mean the animal in full, in relationship to every other being and force in their environment. The most we could do was dissect, regulate, monitor—and ultimately leave them on their own.

Among the things that made the Western Arctic herd unique was size. At its peak, in the early 2000s, the herd had numbered almost five hundred thousand animals, similar to the Bathurst herd at their largest, back in the 1980s. In a year the Western Arctic herd ranged over a territory almost the size of California. Like most migratory caribou they wintered in the boreal forest and began walking north in early spring, toward their calving grounds. In the Western Arctic herd's case, this meant they headed for Alaska's North Slope, the tundra plains at the top of the state that flow down toward the Beaufort Sea. When calving was finished, the herd lingered along the coast, grazing on the plains, harassed almost to madness by mosquitoes, before finally heading south again in autumn.

The scale of their journeys was astonishing. Each year they migrated across nearly a thousand miles of forest, mountains, and tundra, crossing frozen rivers, swimming liquid ones, suffering the ambushes of wolves, bears, and human hunters. Kyle Joly, a biologist with the National Park Service, had used tracking-collar data to show that animals of the Western Arctic outwalked almost every other terrestrial mammal on earth, including the wildebeest of the Serengeti. But while we could track them, Joly told me the enormity of their movements made them obscure.

"So much of their lives are invisible to us," he said. "We usually can't see the changes that happen to them until they're well underway. Until they become really obvious."

Joly was among the worriers, trying to understand the mystery. At his home in northern Colorado, he could slip out his laptop and, over coffee, call up satellite coordinates of collared Western Arctic caribou. They appeared as little blips of pixelated color, plotted on a map. He'd also worked for years in Alaska, traveling in Nunamiut territory and up to the coast and through some of the state's largest national parks. He could summon the herd's location in his mind, too, imagine the landscape and its perils with a decent degree of accuracy. But his experience couldn't tell him *exactly* what was happening to the animals. And even if he were able see them—look down, say, with a drone, in real time—it would only reveal so much.

At a certain point his view became the same as that of

the Tłı̨chǫ, minus the spiritual dimensions: It went hazy in a cloud of variables that included weather, insects, microbes, vegetation, temperature, the movements of humans and other animals, the effects of solar radiation, melting permafrost, oil drilling, mining, the sound of helicopters, of rifle fire, of dynamite. The pathology of the mystery might be related to some of those things, or all of them.

"It's ecology. It's messy. It's complicated," Joly told me. "Right now we're lucky, but is it *just* luck? How long will that luck last?"

Joly was among the first to point me toward Anaktuvuk Pass. In his suggestion I heard a note of urgency—or was it resignation? *Go soon*, he seemed to be saying. *While they're still there.*

IN ANAKTUVUK PASS I RENTED A HOUSE FROM THE local school district that was kept for itinerant teachers. It was small and green and sat on the western edge of town. My bedroom window faced a wall of mountains that ran north–south and that created a kind of funnel, or a highway, along which caribou traveled. Some nights, the northern lights arced up out of those mountains and danced over the house, all green, too, and yellow, like ribbons of bioluminescence in a tropical sea.

That house was the only place in my Arctic travels where I was ever able to entertain visitors. A hunter named Clyde, for instance, who tracked frozen caribou blood across the floor and stayed long enough for it to melt into little red pools. Another hunter named Ben, who once brought an electric saw over to help me cut a pair of antlers from a caribou skull. There was the mayor, Charles Sollie Hugo, and then a group of teenage boys, including William, who traded tales of caribou for stories of New York City. The boys once told me excitedly of the little people, sometimes called *inuguluurak*, or *inukin*, the mischievous dwarfish beings of the tundra who loved to confuse you, play pranks, throw things at you while you were driving snowmobiles, but who were mostly harmless and—now that they thought of it—better left unmentioned.

Once, early in my stay, a kind woman named Casey Edwards took pity on me for the packaged food I'd brought and gave me a ziplock bag stuffed with delicacies: raw caribou backstrap and tongue. Three dark green lines ran down her chin, a tattoo of traditional Iñupiaq design. She was an elder in the local church, a widow, the mother of four. I worried I'd ruin her gift.

"I have no idea how to cook this," I said. "I'll probably fuck it up."

She laughed, a bright, embracing sound. "You can't fuck it up! Just hurry up and cook it."

Casey told me that I could cook it any way I wanted—fry, boil, bake. But I was still intimidated. In the back pantry of the green house I finally found an old crockpot that had been left behind by a teacher who'd come and gone, like they all did, I was told, taking the big paychecks (which were inflated because Anaktuvuk Pass was so remote) for a while and then splitting. I laid the backstrap into the pot with some oil and spices and broth and cooked caribou for the first time.

Since I was using the school's house, I was gently roped into visiting classes ("We never have guests!"), and I was asked to speak about my work to groups of high schoolers, middle schoolers, and even elementary kids, all of whom studied in the same large, rambling building. At first I wasn't sure what to talk about, but soon I settled on wolves. There were white wolves, even blue wolves (their coat had a silver sheen, almost like gunmetal), in the mountains surrounding Anaktuvuk Pass, and quickly I found the students loved talking about them or almost any other animal.

I told them about my time on the Fosheim Peninsula, and I shared photos and stories of One Eye. Everyone laughed when I talked about how she'd ripped up my tent and stolen my pillow. Students told me wolves down here never got that close to humans because they knew they'd get shot. Still, the high-school sports teams were called the Amaguqs (borrowed from *amaguq*, the Iñupiaq word for wolf), and in the lobby stood their mascot: a stuffed white wolf in a smudged glass case.

Whenever I could, I changed the subject to caribou. Then the kids began teaching me.

During quiet moments in class, or while their teachers weren't looking, the older students would show me photos on their mobile phones of caribou they'd caught (*caught* is the word people use to mean killed, or harvested), or of the aurora, or of other animals they'd seen, including wolves and wolverines. They told me which parts of the caribou they liked most to eat and how it was best prepared—dried, fried, chopped into steaks, eaten raw, or fermented.

All of the older students had spent hours, weeks, perhaps even years of their lives on the tundra thinking of caribou. With their families they'd gone camping and hunting during summer recesses, winter breaks, holidays, and, of course, during the autumn caribou migration. Some of the older boys—like William and his cousin, Harry, who together would later catch the caribou that was butchered by students in the classroom—took hunting more seriously. Every day, if the weather was good or even just okay, they'd be out, after school, hunting. William said it was often hard for him to pay attention in class, especially if he sat near a window.

"Why a window?" I asked.

"Because I'm just looking out it the whole time," he said. "Thinking about them. Wondering where they are and what they're up to, where I'm gonna go hunt later."

And it was only springtime.

For most people, autumn was the better hunting season, the most important one. Then, during their return toward the trees, the Western Arctic herds streamed through the valleys of the Brooks Range. The herds of autumn were larger and more cohesive, including males and females of all ages, and, of course, the youngest calves, who'd been born only a few months earlier. In good years the animals had spent the summer grazing on the plains of the North Slope, which meant they arrived to Anaktuvuk Pass in good health—"Looking fat," as Joe Lazare Zoe would've said.

Autumn was the time to catch big bulls, who were prized not for the size of their racks—only recreational hunters cared about those—but for the rich slabs of fat that covered their backs. It was caloric gold. The thickness of such fat was measured in fingers, like liquor. In the old days this was the stuff that helped you survive winter.

Entire families often took to the land during the fall. William said that if it were up to him, he would cut school for the whole season. Some kids, I was told, did just that. People would drive out of town on four-wheelers or six-wheelers called Argos, set up camp, and wait. During the Western Arctic herd's peak, around 2003, when some half million animals were heading south past Anaktuvuk Pass, families might stay on the land for weeks. Sometimes it took that long for all of the caribou to walk by. People filled their refrigerators with meat. Their freezers, too. Like the salmon-fishing tribes of the Pacific coast, the Nunamiut dipped into life's rich current and gave thanks.

No one William's age had been alive during those years. They hadn't seen the sheer mass of the migration, the river of bodies washing through the land, scoring their trails into the soil. But the kids had been hearing about it all their lives, from parents, grandparents, uncles, aunts, distant relatives, in-laws. In a small town where one animal took up so much psychic space, you couldn't avoid the stories. The epic herds of the past ran through everyone's mind like a shared memory.

Practically speaking, it *was* a shared memory. William told me he wished he could've seen it—hundreds of thousands of caribou. He wanted to stand at the edge of such a herd and watch it pass. Dip his hands in the river. Though he never said it, I suspected he wished he could return to the old ways, to the life his grandparents had known. A lot of young Nunamiut I met felt like that, especially young men. They dreamed of the world just gone.

THE NUNAMIUT ARE SOMETIMES CALLED AMERICA'S last nomads because they settled down only around 1950. Before that, they lived in motion, following caribou through the mountains. Their fate had once been so thoroughly tied to the animals that if they suffered, the people did, too, and sometimes the Nunamiut had to find other ways to survive.

A little more than a century ago, most of the Nunamiut had abandoned the mountains and headed to the coasts. They'd done this because the caribou had vanished. No one is certain why the population crashed, though some believe it was due to overhunting: Caribou meat was often sold to the crews of whaling ships that overwintered in the Beaufort Sea. Their appetite for caribou—just like their hunger for whales—was bottomless. Hunting pressure may have decimated the herd during that era.

When their numbers began to rebound in the Brooks Range in the early twentieth century, a few Nunamiut families moved back into the mountains. More soon followed. For a couple of decades they lived as their ancestors had done, hunting and traveling by dogsled in winter, living in tents and houses built of sod in warmer months. During their sojourn on the coasts, the Nunamiut had obtained rifles, developed a taste for coffee, sugar, and tobacco. They'd become Christians. By the middle of the twentieth century, the surpluses of American living convinced several Nunamiut families that it was time for them to join in. "That nomad life was hard," one elder told me. He knew because he'd lived it.

The Nunamiut picked Anaktuvuk Pass as their townsite because of its place along the caribou highway. The word *anatuvuk* itself means "place of many caribou droppings." There was also a lake nearby where floatplanes could land and soon they did, hauling in trade goods. Within a few years the town had an airstrip, a post office, a school. In many ways the town's founding echoed that of nearly every other Indigenous settlement in the Arctic, it just happened later.

The generation of Nunamiut couples who'd made the decision to settle were sometimes called the Founders, and though they were all dead every schoolkid in Anaktuvuk Pass walked past them several times a day. In the lobby outside the school's main office, photographs of them— and of many other deceased elders—had been turned into a kind of memorial mural that ran along the wall. There were couches near the mural and, because there was really no other public space in town, I'd often sit there between classes or while waiting to meet someone.

It was a warm and bright spot, the only place in Anaktuvuk where I could use the internet, and the teachers didn't mind if I made coffee in their lounge a couple of doors down. I would write in my notebook and stare at the faces in the mural, some of whom I recognized from old books. Everyone looked like a celebrity in the black-and-white images, dressed in caribou skins or plaid wool jackets, their faces chiseled and strong and beautiful. Inevitably a kid would

walk by on their way to class and they'd see me looking at
the wall. Then they'd walk up, point out their grandmother,
or great-aunt, and tell me a little story.

Some of the images had been taken by the Norwegian
anthropologist Helge Ingstad, who'd lived with the Nunamiut around the time they'd decided to settle. Other photos
had been taken by family members or various visiting scientists. During that era, the Nunamiut learned that when
you are the "last nomads" you tend to attract *ologists*—
anthropologists, biologists, geologists, archaeologists. The
academics had come in waves, cataloging traditional hunting and crafting methods, gathering the names of animals,
plants, and landforms. They wrote down the grammar of
the language and styles of dress and recorded folktales—
they recorded every detail the Founders would give.

Such research eventually came to feel extractive to
younger Nunamiut (and perhaps to the Founders, too),
who believed they had given much and received little in
return. In the 1950s, Alaska had not yet become a state,
though there was a sense of archival consolidation in the
work of *ologists*, as though the men and women doing it
were appraisers or accountants, cleaning up loose ends. Or
perhaps like prospectors they were taking inventory of every resource Alaska contained to see what it might fetch on
the market.

The decades of objectification, that *lastness*, left a bad
taste with many Nunamiut. After they'd shared their traditional knowledge, after they'd become citizens of a new
state and a young nation, their lives did not necessarily
improve much. In the northern mountains wealth had al-

ways been measured in caribou. This remained true after the Nunamiut settled, but suddenly money also mattered, and Anaktuvuk Pass would never become well-off in that sense.

The oil that was eventually discovered in Prudhoe Bay in the 1960s improved life in some coastal communities and raised the standards of living for many Iñupiat. A little of that cash trickled toward the mountains, to the former no-mads. But they themselves had no mines, no oil deposits, nothing but caribou and a wraparound national park that sometimes felt a like a no-man's land, as though it were de-signed to keep opportunity away.

Anaktuvuk Pass was like so many other small Arctic towns, with its single store, doctorless clinic, one school. There were not many good jobs in town and even the cops, who were white, came from somewhere else. Among the lo-cals bothered by all this was the mayor, Sollie Hugo. I had arrived at the end of the first wave of the Covid-19 pandemic, and to him the disease was merely the latest threat to rise in the south and creep north, more proof of collapsing ecolo-gies, corrosive capitalism, political and religious failure.

The pandemic had also invested Sollie with special emergency power to approve or deny the arrival of visitors. When I initially reached out about coming to Anaktuvuk Pass, his first objective was to ensure that I didn't bring Covid to the town. His second seemed to be to prevent me from taking anything out of it. He warned me before I arrived that the days of handouts to white people were over. Up until the morning I flew north, I wasn't sure he'd actually let me in.

"Don't come here expecting us to just give you our knowledge," he'd said. "We've done enough of that."

ONE OF THE FIRST THINGS YOU NOTICE AFTER YOU arrive in Alaska are the license plates. There are several kinds, but the ones I'm thinking of are among the most common, and simple in such a way that suggests they are the cheapest, or the default. They are bright yellow rectangles adorned with raised blue letters and numbers. Along the bottom is one of Alaska's state slogans: *The Last Frontier.*

The slogan speaks specifically to a certain kind of American, which is to say the sort who believes, correctly, that Alaska was one of the last states to join the Union, and who also probably believes, incorrectly, that for most of the time before statehood, this place was some kind of empty wilderness.

The license plate pissed Sollie off in a way he could not quite put into words, though for a while he tried as we smoked cigarettes on the porch of the tidy little museum in town where he kept an office. Each time he saw one of those plates it was a slap in the face, a jeer, a curse—shit-talk from the rear end of a truck. He felt his anger rise then, he told me. The rage he'd carried for a long time, from his Arctic home to federal prison down south and back again. At least down south the license plates were different. They broadcast vapid stuff—*In God We Trust*, or *You've Got a Friend in Pennsylvania*, maybe *Virginia Is for Lovers.* You couldn't get mad at those. They might have been lies, or just dumb, but they were harmless.

The Alaskan plate, though. If you were an Indigenous person, the state was fucking with you every time it printed one of them. It was lying, Sollie said, right to your face.

"Last frontier my ass."

We stood in silence a few moments, Marlboro Lights barely alive between our fingers. It was so cold the tobacco had no flavor, so dry our smoke vanished almost before it slipped from of our mouths. From the porch we looked across Anaktuvuk Pass to the wall of mountains in the east: a monochrome expanse of snow and ice. It was one of those days where everything was so white it blinded. Sollie was wearing his snowmobile goggles against this stabbing light. They were huge on his small face and curved like a shield over his eyes. He looked like a spaceman. He pointed to black figures in the impossible distance: a line of caribou heading north. I would never have seen them.

Sollie was saying, "Even if you believe the story the archaeologists tell—and I don't—this isn't the final frontier. It was the first. People came over the land bridge from Siberia *to* Alaska. This was the *first* frontier."

Those people, he said, followed caribou out of their world and into this one. He flicked the butt into a coffee can heavy with them. Then he headed back inside to look at the maps that, rather late in life, may yet become his saving grace.

I WAS NOT SURE WHAT TO THINK OF SOLLIE. BEFORE I arrived I learned that he was a registered sex offender. Twenty years earlier he'd been convicted of attempted sexual assault. After I got to town I realized everyone knew what he'd done. He'd spent time in prison, and his story was no secret. Not everyone liked him, but the community had elected him mayor anyway.

Before I traveled to Anaktuvuk Pass I exchanged many emails with Sollie, and pretty quickly the mood got weird. I think at first he mistook me for an *ologist*, and looking back I can't really disagree, though I came on more like a traveling salesman, trading in questions of climate change and animals and the end of the world. In the Canadian Arctic, with Marvin Atqittuq, I'd learned to watch more, ask less. I'd learned not to ask about melting when I was camped on a frozen lake. But I was still a southerner. This was why, Sollie told me later, he'd been reluctant to show me his maps.

One of them was tacked to the wall inside the museum's offices. It was a large topographical map, made of several smaller ones, all laminated and fitted together to show an enormous portion of northern Alaska. On it, in black marker, Sollie had been drawing in the paths used by the Western Arctic herd. He worked from oral histories and the memories of elders, from personal experience and from the reports in the museum collection.

Elsewhere over the plastic skin he'd made notes containing dates, directions, events, names. Here an arrow showed which passes the caribou favored in springtime. There a black circle marked a fishing hole where grayling could be caught. Along a ridge lay the grave of an infamous medicine man. Below the grave, in a valley, were an old homestead, a hunting camp, and the site of the last battle between the Nunamiut and the "Indians" in 1845—a battle the Nunamiut won.

In another room Sollie showed me another map. Arrows indicated where Dall sheep congregated in the high peaks during summer, and how they traveled to lower elevations in the fall. On a certain section of river was one of the most telling notes of all: It revealed a place where the water never froze, even in the coldest winters. In other words, here you might literally save your own life. If the caribou didn't show up, if you were starving, you could come to the river and throw in a net or a spear and catch whitefish.

From this one note on the map it was possible to imagine stories at almost any scale, from that of a solitary wandering hunter, say, to one of a family struggling to survive at the end of a long winter, to the saga of entire people tracking caribou through the mountains. This was the kind of knowledge you earned only by walking the land.

THE SCALE OF THE MAPS WAS ASTOUNDING AND I felt dizzy before them. They were only two-dimensional, but at a glance you saw they contained dozens of other nested dimensions, layer upon layer, line upon line. The maps were indexes and encyclopedias, they were a survivor's guide to the Arctic. Each one contained far more than Sollie alone could have known. It was instead a representation of creation as his people had understood it.

At one point Sollie growled, "It was all a garden. And we tended it."

He was talking about *North America*—tended to,

cultivated, cared for by countless generations of Indigenous people. But I was too distracted to respond. I had heard of such maps, usually rendered digitally. They were called land use maps, and many Indigenous groups compiled them to preserve a record of how their people have used and known landscapes across generations. I had never seen a map like this, though, up close and so detailed. I could not look away. A sensation came over me similar to what I'd experienced when I first met the white wolves—that same breathless thrill and fear.

Here I saw the faintest glimmer of what it might mean to be Indigenous, and of the generations required to truly belong somewhere. The maps were rudimentary and incomplete, but they hinted at how the Nunamiut had become "the people of the land." Here was meaning, gathered and passed down by small groups of people, cycles of learning and sharing. How long had it taken? It was impossible to know, but you felt the weight of it all falling back toward the time when Alaska had been, as Sollie had said, the *first* frontier. When caribou had drawn people from Siberia into Alaska.

In front of the maps, I was also confronted by my own culture's thinness. I felt suddenly homeless. I could think of no similar maps corresponding to my own life—to the suburbs where I'd grown up, or the cities in which I'd lived. It wasn't even possible to make maps like these of my places. They'd all been scraped bare of such stories long ago.

I was suddenly drawn out of my trance by a cough—it was Sollie, redirecting my attention. He wanted me to know there were more.

In an adjacent conference room yet another map spread

over the floor. This one dwarfed the others. It showed the entirety of Arctic Alaska. It was tens of feet wide and long. At the top was Utqiagvik, the Iñupiaq whaling town. To the west was Point Hope; to the southwest the coastal town of Kotzebue. There were not as many notes yet on this map because it was still a work in progress. Sollie told me he planned to add beaver dams to it. The beavers were a new detail, a modern manifestation of climate change. They were creeping northward as the tundra warmed. The dams they built created ponds, and the ponds trapped heat, which then melted the permafrost. Sollie called the beavers evil. He called them *omens*. In some way it was weirdly fitting that he used religious imagery to describe big rodents. The maps, after all, depicted nothing less than life and death, and they were Sollie's magnum opus. To add information, he must kneel before them. To put notes in some interior places he must crawl over their faces, clutching his pen, like a muralist working along the walls of a cathedral.

"I feel compelled to do this," Sollie said. "I *must* do it."

As though it were his penance. His path to redemption.


ON THE WALL OF THE CHAPEL IN THE MOUNTAINS, the only church in Anaktuvuk Pass, there is a painting of Jesus unlike any I have ever seen. I happened to be in the church for the Easter service. In the painting, Jesus rides through the Arctic mountains on the back of a caribou. He is depicted as a white guy, but dressed in traditional Nunamiut clothing. His pants and parka are made of caribou skin, and he holds a traditional skin drum, a *qilaun*, probably also made of caribou. The Lord's face is remarkable because he's not merely smiling but beaming, as though he's just hit the chorus in a truly joyful song. Even if you are like me, a haunter of churches, curious to see inside them all, you have never seen Jesus so happy.

Clyde Morry smiled like that, too.

Out on the tundra northeast of town he always began his hunts with a broad but normal smile—happy enough, in other words, even in deep cold or searing wind. But as soon he shot a cow, *pow*—that smile blew up. Grew holy.

I'd met Clyde the way I met most people in Anaktuvuk Pass: by walking around town. One evening after dark I was headed toward the school when I saw two women in a shed stomping on something. They were Naomi and her daughter-in-law, Miranda, trying to crack the pelvis of a caribou. I stopped to watch while they butchered the rest of the animal and portioned it out into ziplock bags. I noticed small pearlescent grubs wriggling on the smooth inside of the fresh hide.

"Warbles," Naomi said, meaning warble flies, a kind of tundra parasite. "In the summer they lay their eggs on the caribou."

Later the larvae burrow into the animal's skin and spend winter tucked in between layers of fur and flesh. Warbles are a normal part of Arctic life and generally harmless. But they're still sort of gross. I must have made a face, for Naomi smiled and said, "Eat one."

"What?"

"Our elders used to eat them all the time. My dad liked them with peanut butter."

"Have you?"

"I don't like them," she said. "The way they pop. In your mouth." She eyed me, waiting to see if I'd take the dare. Then she invited me in for dinner and told me about her baby brother, Clyde.


ON OUR FIRST HUNT TOGETHER, CLYDE IS CHASING the herd hard.

I cannot keep up. We are on the high plain outside town. He jams the throttle down and his snowmobile surges over the snow, spitting up a fine curtain of white crystals. I turn my own machine this way, that way, flailing over the same frozen ground, but I'm just not that good, and not as hungry as Clyde is for the kill, the pounds of fresh meat, or even for the warmth that will flow up into his hands as he butchers the big caribou. For some reason, even though it is twenty-five degrees, even though the April wind whipping through the pass pushes the chill down further, Clyde never seems to be wearing gloves.

"Just slows me down?" he says later, as though wondering himself.

Everything about Clyde is quick—his basketball game, his work with a skinning knife, his temper. And this is no elegant chase: It's hot pursuit, at breakneck speed. Clyde kicks through a few more turns then skids to a stop, unslings his rifle, and takes aim. There's a blast like a popped balloon, small and hollow against the huge mountains, the empty blue sky. A hundred yards away a cow goes down. The rest of the herd, ten or fifteen mothers and their yearling calves, keep running north but not too far. They sense the worst is over.

Clyde and I drive up to the cow and see his shot has been clean. He slips the knife from his black coveralls, bends over the body. First, he severs her head. The Nunamiut believe that this, and what follows, are the most important steps. He carries the head a little distance away, gently, as though transporting a favorite cat, and places it just as gently in the snow, upside down. The cow's *inua*, her soul, may now escape and fly to the spirit world. There, the Keeper of the Caribou, a being who carries his heart in his hand to show that he can never die, will comfort the cow's soul and send her to earth again in a new body.

"Thank you for this meat!" Clyde shouts into the blue void. In the distance the rest of the little herd turns to stare. "It won't be wasted!"

This is the cycle of respect and renewal. It is what you do each time to guarantee the caribou will keep coming. Clyde is thirty-six years old and it is what he knows, what he was taught, and it is, too, what he teaches his two children. After the head is set, Clyde begins butchering. Quick sharp strokes. Slick red hands. When his fingers get cold he shakes them and blows on them—"Hoo-wee!"—and pushes them against the carcass to soak up some fading heat. When the quarters of meat are finally stacked on his sled, Clyde says, "Maybe I'll put on some gloves for the drive home."

He does, and drives back to Anaktuvuk Pass at a much safer speed. This is not to say he drives slowly. Clyde is mindful not to let the meat freeze—that would just make the finer cutting, the portioning and bone-stomping, harder for Naomi. But this time, going home, I manage to keep up. Even, once, to pass him. As I do, I notice Clyde's beaming.

He has no job but this, he wants no job but this. Hunting is how Clyde provides for his big extended family, including Naomi and her children and her and Clyde's recently widowed father. Tonight at home there will be plenty of food and plenty of people gathering to eat it.

Clyde's dad, Mark, presiding over the meal and the crowd, will ask me, "Did you see him turn the head over?"

"Yes," I'll say.

The elder will nod. "Don't forget."


CLYDE AND I GO OUT TOGETHER A FEW MORE TIMES, and each trip unfolds the same way. Not too many other people are out hunting these days; it seems they're waiting for the cold to slacken, or perhaps they're waiting until autumn, when hunting is easier. I wonder if we'll encounter William and his posse of teen hunters, but then I remember they're in school. Clyde's dad had told me once that there was no weapon more effective than school for killing a nomad's spirit. What it meant was that we had the land and the animals to ourselves.

One day, I finally work up the courage to answer Naomi's dare. I pick a warble larvae off a fresh caribou carcass, toss it into my mouth. There is the pop she'd warned me of—like a briny grape. It is possibly the most awful thing I have ever tasted. Clyde screams, "You fucking did it! I can't believe you did it!"

He slaps my back like a football player. When I ask

how many he's eaten, he just says, "None, dude. That shit's nasty."

On another day, Clyde's driving all crazy, chasing a herd, carving impossible loops in the snow like a misfired rocket. I don't know where he'll turn next, so I follow best I can, close but not too close, and when he suddenly stops, I'm still in motion. It's too late for me to veer away as he raises his rifle.

He jerks up the barrel and starts cussing and bellowing. *Never fucking drive in front of me when I'm shooting!* The suddenness of his rage is frightening, and for a moment I feel for his kids. But then the lesson clicks. Next time I'll follow well behind and give whatever room he requires. I am grateful that one of Clyde's qualities is the flash-bang nature of his anger—it doesn't last long.

Yet another day, after our final hunt together, Clyde's bent over, butchering the old cow. Her ribs are open to the sky. Clyde is thinking of dinner. His dad had wanted a female; he believed they tasted better. And Clyde, a son seeking affection, had worked hard to get this one.

Suddenly he recoils and bolts upright.

"What the fuck?"

We peer down. The cow's insides are speckled with little gray pustules. Tumors. Clyde is disgusted. He says something about how this happens more often these days, but mostly he's pissed that he's wasted his time, wasted gas and ammo. I notice several warbles scrunching around on the cow's skin like fat little accordions and I gag. Clyde spits. He abandons the carcass in a crimson heap on the gleaming snow. Next day the pile will still be there, surrounded by the paw prints of frustrated wolves who arrived too late, after dusk, after all the meat froze stiff.

Later that afternoon I ask if Clyde's really seen a rise in the number of cancerous animals coming through Anaktuvuk Pass. My question sounds unusually official, the ask of an *ologist*, and Clyde side-eyes me. Yes, he says, though with less conviction. He's still angry about the hunt, but soon the anger sinks into something else. The *herd*, he says, sounding hurt. It's sick.

LIKE ROY JUDAS IN THE TŁĮCHǪ HOMELAND, CLYDE learned to hunt his tribe's caribou during their peak years, when the herd was at its largest. As with Roy, Clyde had seen real *abundance*, and it meant he could recognize its opposite. Even though it seemed plenty of caribou were still coming into the country, Clyde thinks something is wrong and he is deeply troubled. He tells me that in some years, very few caribou now trickle through the mountains. In others they arrive late, or don't come at all. Bulls aren't as big as they used to be, they don't pack as much coveted fat on their backs. Fewer calves seem to survive. And sometimes the animals taste different, too, which is one of the most disturbing details of all.

These kinds of anecdotal evidence are hard to measure, especially for any uninitiated outsider. In Alaska, the testimony of Indigenous people about wild animals, water, plants, and other things the state has classified as "public resources" has often been treated with circumspection, sometimes hostility. Esther Hugo, the president of the

Nunamiut tribe, a small woman with long gray hair, once told me that she'd gone to meeting after meeting with state officials, often flying to faraway towns and cities to raise the alarm about the Western Arctic herd's decline. In her mind, much of the cause was "head hunters," sportsmen who pay outfitters a lot of money to hunt big bull caribou. These hunters disrupted migration patterns, she said, and didn't follow the ancient rules, like freeing the caribou *inua*, or another important one that involved letting the first animals in a herd pass by unharmed. This tradition is commonly held to ensure that caribou keep migrating over the same ground, year after year.

Esther told me that state officials hardly listened to her anymore. They'd see her walk up to the microphone at a public meeting and roll their eyes. When I asked a government biologist about this, he sighed and didn't deny it. "Poor Esther. She does come to a lot of meetings."

The man was sympathetic. He said he understood how much the caribou meant to the Nunamiut. But in his mind there was no way, mathematically speaking, that trophy hunters could have such an outsized effect on a still very large herd of caribou. There simply weren't enough sport hunters, he said. And they only hunted bulls, not cows, who are far more valuable in terms of reproduction.

"I think maybe what the Nunamiut feel is helplessness," the biologist said. Then he lowered his voice, "What did they think was gonna happen? You turn from the walkingest people in the world into people who sit and wait for caribou. Your ancestors *never* did anything like that."

This kind of disconnect was common everywhere I'd traveled in the Arctic. It was a line of dissonance drawn between the white world, the world of science and politics, and the Indigenous one, which relied on other ways of seeing, assessing, and negotiating reality. Clyde never went to any of the meetings where this line cut through the room, where it could be seen in the queues of Indigenous people waiting to speak before boards or commissions that were, often enough, made up of white people.

But in Clyde's case, things were different. His concerns carried like an echo, and I'd heard the same details from other hunters, from elders, and even from state biologists and wildlife managers. This last group repeated Clyde's observations and worries about caribou health, but in their own peculiar language of satellite data, aerial survey numbers, and mortality rates. The point was this: Whatever was actually *causing* it, no one doubted anymore that the Western Arctic herd was in trouble. The questions were now of another order. Would it stop, for example. And if not, what then?

*What then* was the sharpest question, piercing to the heart for the Nunamiut, just as it was for the Tłı̨chǫ.

The tumors we'd found inside the caribou earlier that day seemed, to Clyde, a kind of omen, like Sollie's beavers. It was impossible to separate that rot from the rest of his life which, that afternoon, seemed achingly thin. His wife had left him. He had no job. His sisters gave him money for gas and sometimes he borrowed his dead mother's snowmobile without permission from his grieving father, and that just made everything messy. Sometimes ugly.

What Clyde had, what he clung to, was hunting. Would he have to stop, he wondered. And if so, what then.

"I wish we could go back to the old days," he says.

Clyde's face is kind and round, still a boy's face, above a boy's hunched shoulders. He'd been the baby in his big family, doted on by his mother and sisters. He told me he'd been the one to find his mother dead on the floor of the house he grew up in. She had truly been one of the last of the nomads. Born on the land, born in motion. He felt like her life made his—made everyone's—look still. Like they were standing around in a classroom, waiting for something to happen. Hearing about life secondhand.

The last time I saw him, Clyde gave me a piece of worked stone, a relic he'd found in the valley, in the earth. He liked to dig for things his ancestors left behind and he had a reputation for finding incredible objects. The tool he gave me might have been hundreds of years old, or thousands. It was gray and black, its edge still sharp. Possibly it had been a scraper, used to clean caribou hides. Clyde told me that he always carried something like that in his pocket whenever he went out hunting. It reminded him, he said. It was good luck.


A FEW MONTHS LATER I'M STANDING ON THE BANK OF the Kobuk River in Western Alaska, watching a young caribou try to swim the dark water. It isn't going well. The river is a jumble of floating ice and the buck is taking a beating. Rafts of ice spin down the current and clobber him, shove him under. I can hear him cough and splutter.

On the shore stand a group of his less daring companions. They are waiting to see how it will turn out. If he makes it maybe they'll try, though at this rate the buck seems like he'll become another casualty of the warming world. A chunk of ice, another dunking—I lose sight of the buck in the jagged white mess.

I am about two hundred miles southwest of Anaktuvuk Pass, at a place called Onion Portage, which lies inside the remote and enormous Kobuk Valley National Park. Deep forests of spruce and birch line the valley, and nearer the water stand willow thickets dense as walls. To the east, the Jade Mountains rise and flare white under fresh snow. It's late October and I may well have the park, nearly three thousand square miles of wilderness, to myself.

I've come to say goodbye. From here my journey will turn toward other stories in Greenland and Europe, and I'd wanted to be alone with the caribou to see them on their own terms as I'd once done with the wolves. When I asked around about where I might do this, everyone pointed me here, even Sollie Hugo—Onion Portage is prominently marked on his maps. And they were right: I am surrounded. Western Arctic caribou stamp through the forest and along the riverbank. They bed down in the meadows nearby. At night they sprint past my tent and shake the earth, an avalanche of hooves. There are hundreds of them here, perhaps thousands, all waiting to cross the Kobuk. And there are other beings, too. Wolves who sit below my camp at night and howl. A brown bear who visits in daytime while I'm out hiking. He leaves enormous paw prints outside my door and even larger turds on the trails we share, but he's neighborly. Unlike One Eye, he leaves my stuff alone.

The river is the last obstacle in the Western Arctic herd's autumn migration, which makes this one of the greatest human-caribou convergence zones in North America. Archaeologists have shown that for ten thousand years, caribou have been funneling toward Onion Portage, and for at least that long human hunters have arrived to meet them. It has been a regular appointment, a correspondence kept across an astonishing gulf of time. The depth of the story echoes, though now another one is growing louder. These days the hunters still come, but the caribou are often late. Sometimes they don't show up at all.

Biologists tell me it's the heat: in our time the Alaskan autumn lasts longer, which delays both the migration and the freeze up. Warming is also changing the landscape. An archaeologist who excavated here in the 1960s told me he can hardly recognize the site anymore. There are too many new trees. What it all means for caribou is that they more often reach a river in transition—not exactly liquid, not fully frozen. The young buck is learning just how dangerous this in-betweenness can be. Out on the river he takes a few more hits and then gives up. He struggles back to shore and rejoins his companions. Together they turn toward me, lift their chins in disapproval, and march into the trees. *Click, click, click* go their hooves. The scent of their musk is sharp, sweet, strong.

During the days I spend at Onion Portage, one overwhelming feeling is grief for all that seems to be passing away. Even though I'm a southerner I feel it, a silence spreading beneath our modern clamor. I have now tracked caribou around the north for several years, and I don't feel any closer to understanding what's happening to them. If they are—as I have come to believe—a manifestation of the landscape itself, then it's hard to see past the shadows while their numbers shrink and the land changes and the old correspondence crumbles.

And yet. Before coming here I learned that some herds living nearer the Arctic coast, including one called Porcupine, may be holding out against whatever is eating away at their inland cousins. The Porcupine may even be increasing. I take heart, too, in the work researchers are doing with "caribou cameras"—small-battery powered devices mounted to tracking collars. For the first time these cameras offer glimpses into the secret lives of caribou, when they're out on the land and far from our sight. Many of the images of daily caribou life, I'm told, are boring. Some, though, capture dramas—life-and-death struggles with wolves, for example. Scientists can also see what they're eating, what they're drinking. In these new views may lie clues to the great mystery.

I share this partly to remind myself that beyond our worry and plans, life goes on for the herds. They are not just victims, not merely supporting characters in a human show. For all their apparent vulnerability, caribou are survivors. They escaped the Pleistocene extinctions some thirteen thousand years ago. Their numbers have risen and fallen for as long as we can remember. To imagine them condemned is to deny them any agency of their own, and the Nunamiut (as well as the Tłįchǫ) remember that they always have a refuge: they can abandon us here and return to their own country, where the Keeper of the Caribou waits for them, holding his heart in his hands.

There is hope, then, for them. And we must remember to be hopeful, too.

After the frustrated caribou have left me alone on the riverbank, I stand awhile in the enormous silence and try to envision the future. What will happen to the caribou? What could our world look like without them? For all my trying, it isn't caribou that eventually come into mind. Instead, I remember one afternoon near the end of my stay in Anaktuvuk Pass. A squad of boys came over to visit me at the little green house. There was William and his cousin Harry, Harry's brother Xavier, another cousin named Harlin, a kid named Daniel. They'd just returned from a hunt and wanted to tell me about it. They were covered in blood and beaming. They'd spent hours on the land searching for caribou, loving them in that way, keeping up the human end of the relationship.

In the end they'd caught three. They butchered the animals and delivered the meat to house-bound elders. Harry had cut two fingers while skinning an animal and he'd needed six stitches. Daniel had a red gash over his right eye where he'd "scoped" himself—he'd held his rifle too close to his face and been bashed by its recoil. Little injuries, big badges of honor. I made mac-n-cheese from a box for the boys and they sprawled around the living room, laughing and eating and teasing each other. I could not remember ever seeing teens so pleased or proud, so intent on the gifts of animals.

# THE LOST COLONY

*Grøenland*

I N THE CEMETERY AT THE END OF THE WORLD THERE are not enough women and children. In fact there are hardly any at all.

Dorthe Pedersen spreads her arms wide and says, "We don't know where they are, but they're not *here*."

She is a small woman with bright blond hair, a fringe of bangs across her forehead, a smudge of dirt along her chin. In one hand she holds a trowel. She stands in a shallow pit near the edge of a fjord in southern Greenland. She is almost up to her ankles in bodies, centuries-old bodies from the time when Vikings lived here.

But these crumbling dead are mostly adult men, as far as anyone can still tell, as far as age and sex matter across such a span of time. For now, it matters this way: Men did not live here alone like monks. In an excavation of this kind, which is unfolding in a medieval graveyard that once sat at the heart of a Viking colony, you would expect the dead to include many more women and children, who made up the other two-thirds or so of the population.

For now they are missing. From this and many of the other Viking cemeteries on the enormous island. Their absence leaves one of the more glaring holes in a saga we are slowly coming to understand, one that tells us not only of the past but also something about what it means to face a frightening future.

I ask Dorthe where the missing might be. She smiles and shrugs. Maybe a little to the left, maybe a little to the right. She waves her trowel at the meadow rolling down to a broad fjord, which glitters blue and still under the warm August sun. The missing might be anywhere. And it puzzles her, this difference in burials, not least because she is a woman and the mother of four sons. Where are the others like her, like her family? Why are they not here? What was so different in the fourteenth or fifteenth century, when the bodies at her feet seem to have been buried?

These were medieval people, she tells me. They didn't see the world in the same ways we do.

At times it's hard even to imagine their perspective—their motivations and conversations, the ways faith or experience shaped them. This of course is why Dorthe digs, why she is here. This is what archaeologists do: They try to give our imaginations a little more to work with. Try to build up firmer ground, present a case, dispel some darkness. They try, ultimately, to connect old stories to our modern ones.

Sometimes it works, sometimes it doesn't. They are up against a lot these days. It is 2022, the strange interregnum between Donald Trump's first term as president of the United States, when he offered to buy Greenland, and his second term, when he began threatening to simply annex it. The Covid-19 pandemic is not quite over and may never really end. In Europe, Russia's invasion of Ukraine continues. Against the urgency of each day's news, Arctic history can seem thin, even undifferentiated. One long cold line stretching unbroken from a hazy past of nomads and animals up to the moment white explorers arrived and wrenched everything into the modern era. Not nearly as many people study the Arctic past as, say, study the bright and obvious monuments of Egypt. But the Greenland Vikings, or Norse, as they're often called, have much to tell us and their story deserves a better hearing, because it looks so much like our own. More than five hundred years ago, they faced many of the same chaotic forces we do, and they did not survive.

Down in the pit, Dorthe bends back to the work. Two of her excavators, Rikke Olsen and Sara Elleskov, are cleaning off a pair of skeletons buried so close together that their bones seem almost to have fused. In a corner beside them, another excavator, Birte Olsen (not related to Rikke), brushes soil from the skull of a third man. His bones are the color of tea and the consistency of "wet biscuit." Wormlike roots push out from his eye sockets and mouth. His teeth are a mess. He is barely more than a stain in the soil and what's left of his countenance suggests shock, as though he were stunned to find himself in daylight after nearly a millennium underground.

Dorthe mentions that the men her team has found, more than two dozen so far, were buried facing east, toward the spot medieval Christians believed Jesus would appear at the Second Coming. So perhaps it's not the light that's surprising this skeleton so much as it is the company. Dorthe's team is three female Danes and one nonbinary Greenlander.

She says, "This is definitely not the resurrection he had in mind."


NO ONE KNOWS WHAT HAPPENED TO THE GREENLAND Norse. Their finale remains unwritten, and their fate is one of the most alluring puzzles of the far north. What we understand is that their culture apparently began to unravel in the 1300s and rapidly fell apart about a century later. By the middle of the fifteenth century, the Norse had vanished. Climate change was probably a driving force behind their ruin (though the changes they faced were very different from ours), and there were likely others, too, perhaps including warfare, economic collapse, or social upheaval. The details, though, are obscure; the causes probably entangled. Almost certainly the Norse stared into the future and saw their world coming to an end. But that's getting ahead of the story.

The first Norse settlers arrived in Greenland in about AD 986, sailing west from Iceland and following Erik Thorvaldsson, who is better known to us as Erik the Red. The people who journeyed with him across the sea belonged to a culture that was expert in the art of cold-weather colonization. Their ancestors had learned to thrive in Iceland, discovered the Faeroe Islands, pushed into the Shetlands, and settled in many other remote regions of the North Atlantic and northern Europe. Greenland added a fresh dimension to their explorations: At the time it was, to Europeans, the very edge of the known world, the farthest frontier on the storm-plagued sea.

Darkness and distance had never stopped the Norse. And they may have been encouraged, too, by a period of relative warmth and mild weather, which seems to briefly have reduced sea ice and calmed the North Atlantic's ferocious weather.

Today we call this phase the Medieval Climate Anomaly, and while the Norse surely appreciated better weather, the journey remained long—a roughly thousand-mile transit from western Iceland to the fjords of southern Greenland. The Norse sailed in slender open boats with square woolen sails and wooden oars. They packed aboard these longships everything they believed necessary to remake their lives on the frontier, from cattle, horses, and sheep to tools, weapons, and slaves, or *thralls*.

Some of the Norse were likely Christian, early Catholics to be precise, while others probably still worshipped older gods like Thor, Odin, and Freya. Their ships were robust, the crews experienced, but surely the passengers prayed as they sailed, for the sea was still the sea. According to *The Saga of the Greenlanders*, one of the few medieval sources to record stories of this period, twenty-five ships left Iceland during the initial exodus, and only fourteen survived the crossing.

IT'S OFTEN SAID THAT THE NORSE, OR EVEN ERIK HIMSELF, *discovered* Greenland. They didn't, though for a while at the beginning they may have believed they had landed first. Soon they appear to have discovered relics left by earlier people. Today we call these people the Tuniit (or the Dorset), and they'd arrived long before the Norse, traveling from the other direction: eastward, out of what is now Arctic Canada.

The Tuniit are extinct, and they don't seem to be related to the Inuit, the Indigenous people who today comprise nearly all of Greenland's population. But when the Norse showed up the Tuniit were not gone yet: Research has shown that they had abandoned the southern parts of the island and retreated northward. This was possibly because they were an Arctic-adapted people, and while the climate anomaly made the fjords inviting to the Norse, it grew too warm for the Tuniit. They became, in other words, medieval climate emigrants.

The Norse don't seem to have been too curious about the Tuniit, at least not in the beginning. They were simply pleased to find uninhabited space. The frontier was vast, a maze of dazzling, serpentine fjords lined with emerald tundra that, in some ways, evoked familiar landscapes in Iceland and northern Norway.

The meadows were rich with bilberry and Labrador tea, low birches, willows and junipers, and other species the settlers knew. There were common mosses and lichens, small herds of caribou, foxes and big Arctic hares. The sea was busy with seals and whales, and at the top of almost every fjord sat a glacier. Ice was nothing new to the Norse. Though they were not quite as cold-adapted as the Tuniit and other Arctic groups, they understood ice as part of life in the far north. They probably didn't think much of it until many decades later, when the climate began to cool and the ice started creeping down the mountains.

Within a generation of Erik's landing, dozens of farms had been established in the southern fjords. The area was called Vatnaherfi, which in Old Norse means something like Lake District—the colonial heartland. They built robust homes of stone and roofed them with peat. They raised enormous byres, or barns, using stones so large that they still cast cold shadows on a hot summer day. They may have built irrigation systems, and they grazed animals across green meadows that they labored to improve, working manure into the soil by hand. There were churches, too, and perhaps pagan sites of prayer, and many mysterious structures whose purposes are still unknown.

TODAY ARCHAEOLOGISTS COUNT SOME FIVE HUNDRED farms in Vatnaherfi. The Norse also called this Eystribygð, the Eastern Settlement. There are more farms farther north, near the modern capital of Nuuk, in what was named Vestribygð, the Western Settlement. The density of farms, especially in the Eastern Settlement, shows the Norse knew how to use every available surface in the narrow zone between the glaciers and the sea. It also suggests that farmers enjoyed at least some kind of success in adapting their European methods to Greenland's meager soil.

This, too, wasn't new to the Norse. Even at the height of their medieval infamy for raiding and pillaging— for being *Vikings*—the Norse were mostly farmers and largely pastoral. They focused on sturdy cattle, long-maned horses, sheep, goats, and a variety of crops. While Greenland was probably too cold for most domesticated plants, the Norse may have been able to coax a few crops from the tundra during the short summers, in sun-favored places sheltered from the wind. Ancient grains of barley have been found here (though it's not clear if they were grown or imported), and surely these, in sufficient quantity, would've tempted thirsty Norse to brew North America's first beer.

The Norse also traveled far beyond their new homes. Evidence found on the Canadian island of Newfoundland shows they made at least one and possibly several voyages to the North American mainland sometime around AD 1000. They probably cruised up the west coast of Greenland during the summer, too, hunting walruses in what is now called Disko Bay. Walrus hunting soon became an important part of the Norse economy, and tusks were shipped back to Europe where they fed a market in luxury goods that included chess pieces, thrones, crucifixes, and ornate blade handles. Sometimes the walrus boats seem to have traveled even farther, perhaps all the way to Melville Bay or even the east coast of Ellesmere Island—to within a hundred and fifty miles of the Fosheim Peninsula where, centuries later, I would visit the white wolves.

These were incredible journeys. They show the Norse were willing to brave ice-choked seas and extreme weather more than a thousand miles beyond the heartland of the Eastern Settlement. And unlike the southern fjords, these Arctic places were not uninhabited. It was out there, along

One Eye (right) and her sister. It isn't clear what caused One Eye's injury, though it's possible her eyeball was knocked inward during a hunt, by a kick from a musk ox.

A herd of musk oxen pull into defensive formation against the wolves, who sit watching on the hill in the background.

*All photos were taken by the author, unless otherwise noted.*

With little meat left on this musk ox carcass, the pack will soon need to hunt again. Research suggests that most wolf hunts fail, which means a family can go days, sometimes weeks, between big meals.

After a game of keep-away on a frozen pond, one of the pups sits with his prize: a puck of ice. Play is a crucial aspect of the pups' development—one way by which they learn to *become* wolves.

The "gargoyle" den on the Fosheim Peninsula overlooks a vast sweep of open tundra and prime musk oxen pasture. In a niche within this outcrop, many generations of wolf mothers have likely birthed their pups.

One of the pack crosses a frozen pond at dusk. By mid-September, when this photograph was taken, most ponds on the Fosheim are lidded with ice, a portent of the deep cold soon to come.

Lost on the tundra, the pack's four pups howl for help. Such calls can be heard for several miles over the open tundra, and soon enough the older wolves returned to gather up the pups.

The town of Gjoa Haven—named for Roald Amundsen's ship, *Gjøa*—lies in the traditional territory of an Inuit tribe called the Netsilingmiut, "the people of the seal." Their name for the area is Uqsuqtuq.

Two members of the 1st Canadian Ranger Patrol Group check GPS coordinates before heading north out of Gjoa Haven. Both men wear traditional clothing—Adam in pants made of polar bear hide, Anthony in a caribou skin parka—mixed with modern stuff that wasn't nearly as warm, but *namuktuk*—good enough for now.

On the frozen sea south of town, hunters Paul Ikuallaq and Ikey Nashaooraitook pause to talk about where the caribou might be. After many hours spent stalking the sea and tundra the men went home with only a ptarmigan to show for their effort.

Jacob Atqittuq sits by the stove in his tent atop a frozen lake called Kakivaktorvik, "the place to fish with a spear." Jacob was born in the 1940s and grew up on the tundra along Canada's Back River. Even after moving to Gjoa Haven in adulthood he never bothered to learn much English and kept close to traditional ways.

Members of the Tłı̨chǫ Nation's Boots on the Ground program scan for Bathurst caribou near the top of Koketi, also called Contwoyto Lake. From left: Janet Rabesca, Tyanna Steinwand, and Joe Lazare Zoe. (*Credit Katie Orlinsky*)

Tundra flows down to an inlet along the shore of Koketi, which means roughly "lots of camps by the water." The seventy-mile-long lake lies at the far eastern edge of Tłįchǫ territory and connects the Northwest Territories and Nunavut. Two major migratory caribou herds, the Bathurst and the Beverly, spend summers near the lake.

Roy Judas relaxes after finally finding a small herd of Bathurst caribou near the end of a two-week search for the animals.

Joe Zoe raises his arms to mimic antlers—an old hunters' trick that often catches the attention of distant caribou and lures them closer.

The town of Anaktuvuk Pass sits in the Brooks Range of northern Alaska. It is home to the Nunamiut, "the people of the land," who have been called America's last nomads. *Anaktuvuk* means "lots of caribou droppings," and hints at the regular passage of the animals through this remote country.

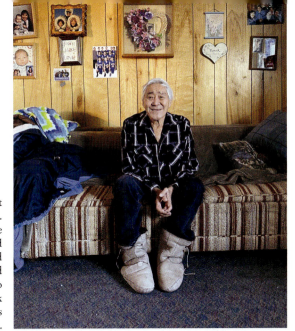

Elder Raymond Paneak at his home in Anaktuvuk. Paneak was one of the few Nunamiut who could remember nomadic life, and he often spoke about it and taught traditional skills to community youth. Paneak died a few months after this photo was taken.

A small herd of caribou gathers outside Anaktuvuk in the early phase of the spring migration. By June, tens of thousands of caribou will have moved north onto the coastal plains above Beaufort Sea, where pregnant females will give birth on the same calving grounds used by generations of their ancestors. (*Credit Katie Orlinsky*)

This young female caribou was "caught" by students in Anaktuvuk's only school and later hauled into a classroom in preparation for a workshop on traditional butchery. Led by elder Raymond Paneak, students learned how to cut and name each part of the animal.

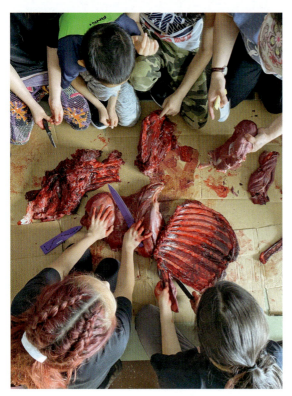

Students from kindergarten to high school took part in the butchery workshop, dividing meal-sized portions of meat into plastic bags that were later given to elders in the community.

Clyde Morry cracks a caribou leg on the tundra outside town. Clyde was one of the few hunters working the spring migration during my visit, and he went out regularly, alone. The caribou he caught fed his large extended family.

After killing a caribou, Nunamiut hunters remove the head and then turn it upside down so that the animal's *inua*, or soul, may return to the spirit world. There it will be comforted and cared for, and ultimately joined with another body. Then it will return to earth to replenish the herd. This shot was taken after the ritual was observed.

A view of the village of Igaliku, overlooking the fjord of the same name. During the Norse era, this site was known as Garðar, and was home to a large farmstead. In the early twelfth century a cathedral was built here, and Garðar was established as the first bishopric on the North American continent.

Dorthe Pedersen (left), Birte Olsen (middle), and Rikke Olsen excavate a medieval cemetery near the Garðar cathedral. After several weeks of work the team unearthed more than thirty skeletons, most apparently of adult men. Researchers have not yet found similarly grouped burials of women and children.

A child's skull found in the excavation—one of only two. Pedersen and her team planned to use their discoveries to help construct an overview of the Norse population in the fjords, including a finer estimate of how many people lived in the colony.

This stylized horse, small enough to fit in the palm, was discovered in a midden, or trash heap, at a Norse farm not far from Igaliku. It may have been a child's toy, and the shape, along with the carefully carved mane—likely meant to evoke knots or braids—suggests an aesthetic that connected settlers here to the mother culture of Norse Europe.

The ruins of Hvalsey church, about ten miles south from Igaliku. The church is believed to have been built around AD 1300 atop an older church. Its massive, well-fitted walls suggest that stonemasons from Europe—possibly Scotland—were employed to build it. Some of the last news ever heard from the Norse colony in Greenland originated at this site: a wedding in 1408, and a witch burning sometime earlier.

Thomas Nilsen and Georgii Chentemirov of *The Barents Observer* pose with a portrait of the late last leader of the Soviet Union, Mikhail Gorbachev.

Hoping to reframe history, two men hang a portrait of slain Ukrainian soldier Oleksandr Matsievskyi on the base of a statue commemorating the Red Army's liberation of Kirkenes from the Nazis during World War II. Matsievskyi was apparently executed in Ukraine in 2022 by invading Russian forces and he soon became a national symbol of resistance. An epitaph on the portrait reads, "Russia make no mistake about it; you are the Nazis now."

A Norwegian soldier holds a German army helmet, one of countless World War II–era relics found along the Norway-Russia border. After invading the Soviet Union across this region in 1941, the Nazis were chased back over the frontier in 1944 by Red Army troops who went on to liberate northern Norway.

A view of the Norway-Russia border near the Norwegian border station called Korpfjell. The wooden planks laid down over soggy tundra allow patrolling soldiers easier passage during the spring melt.

A cross towers over dunes along the Norway-Russia border, not far from the shore of the Barents Sea.

A rainbow falls over Russia beyond the "German bridge," which was built by the Nazis and left mostly intact by Norway and Russia. "All you need to do," a soldier told me, "is throw down a few planks. Then you could drive over it."

the cold edges, that the Norse may have met remnant groups of Tuniit. Later they almost certainly met the Inuit, who crossed over into Greenland from the continent in about the year 1200.

For me, these meetings are fascinating because they are so mysterious. Imagine them—three peoples, sighting each other in the distance, moving along the shore or between blocks of floating ice, trying to get a better look at one another. We can see so little about them and their encounters. We don't know, for example, how the Norse and the Inuit got along. Of the Tuniit even less is known, though around this time we begin to see their culture fading away. They may have watched from the sidelines as the two ascendant groups clashed or bonded or both.

By the time the Inuit and the Norse met, their extremely adaptable cultures had spread over significant portions of the globe. The Inuit were part of a larger cultural and linguistic family that reached across half the Arctic, from what is now Alaska to the northeast coast of Greenland. It would've been possible to travel across that vast territory of ice and tundra without ever leaving a world of shared stories, values, and languages. The Norse, for their part, had spread in a similar way, but in the other direction. You might have headed east from Greenland's southern fjords and, speaking only Norse, gone all the way to what is now Russia, then turned south toward Constantinople and pushed on toward Baghdad.

These exploring peoples made astounding journeys, and yet something even simpler and more profound was unfolding in Greenland than the Norse, Inuit, and Tuniit

could see. They represented two streams of human migration that had emerged from Africa some sixty thousand or
more years earlier. One of those streams headed north into
Europe, the other flowed east into Asia, both populating
the earth on their ways. After thousands of generations,
the streams finally met again in the Arctic, under the midnight sun, having carried the earthly dreams of our ancestors as far as they could go.

WHILE I TRAVELED THROUGH THE REMAINS OF THE
Norse colony, I often thought of science fiction, and how
much they appeared like space explorers, settlers of new
moons or solar systems. It's not a perfect analogy. We know
that for generations ships traveled between Europe and
Greenland, hauling critical supplies of lumber and iron. We
know that people traveled back and forth; we know that
Catholic bishops arrived to ensure the salvation of souls,
or at least the payment of tithes. Excavations of cemeteries
have shown that Greenlanders even tried to keep up with
European fashions.

All this is to say that after crossing the dark, deadly
expanse of the sea and traveling up into the frigid white
spaces of the far north, the colonists did what colonists
always do, even in sci-fi novels: They kept looking back.
As they struggled to build new lives in a new world, their
gaze was fixed on the old one, right up until the end. You
see it in what they made and carried. You see it in what
they left behind.

I am thinking specifically of a horse.

This horse is carved of dark wood and small enough to fit in the palm of my hand. When an archaeologist shows it to me, in a storage room in a museum in Nuuk, I can instantly tell that whoever made it centuries ago was careful, discerning. The horse is shapely, almost serpentine. You can still see elegant braids notched into the mane. It doesn't represent an actual horse—it's not realism—but a stylized ideal. Holding it in my hand I think of the Trojan horse. It had been found in a midden, an ancient trash heap, outside a ruined Viking house. The archaeologist guessed it had been made for a child. He did not know why it had been tossed into the midden.

Because Greenland's tundra did not support trees of any size, the wood may have come from Europe, or perhaps from the coast of what is now Canada. For me the braids are the most striking and bittersweet detail because they suggest a sense of *home*. Of culture. In the braids you see reflected notions of beauty and order, and also a kind of hope. If this was a toy, it was also a teaching tool. It said, *Here is how a horse is supposed to look. This is how you will braid the mane one day.* It was also a kind of totem: It spoke to the child of a future in which there would be horses, and pastures, and hay.

There are still horses in Greenland. They aren't descended from the lost colony, though they offer a glimpse of the small herds that roamed here hundreds of years ago. You come across them now and then in the rolling meadows. The ones I saw were mud-spattered and wild-maned. They looked very happy. I saw them first as I hiked over the hump of a peninsula in the rain toward a tiny town that today is called Igaliku, though the Norse knew it as something else. To them it was Garðar, and it had once been the home of Catholic bishops.

On that rainy August morning, I followed a dirt road through gleaming, sheep-flecked pastures. Big bales of hay had been wrapped in white plastic and left to sit, like giant marshmallows. We think of this island as a kingdom of ice and it is, but at some point every summer visitor to the southern fjords sees why Erik the Red named this place Grøenland. When he arrived, during the Medieval Climate Anomaly, temperatures in the fjords were only a bit cooler than they are today. The tundra in high summer probably looked rich and inviting, much as it does in Canada's barren lands. The color always conceals a hardness, though—permafrost or solid, impenetrable rock. In Greenland you find both, and I knew the pastures I was crossing were manufactured, a legacy from the Norse. These were the meadows they'd worked hard to terraform—to improve and maintain. I was hiking along their ghost road, passing through their phantom fields.

I REACHED IGALIKU IN THE EVENING, SOAKED AND cold. By morning the sky had cleared and I walked into the center of town looking for Dorthe Pedersen and her team. At the tiny hotel a woman told me I couldn't miss them: just follow the sound of laughter. I went outside and heard nothing—the town lay utterly still and silent above a glittering blue fjord. Then I heard a metallic *clang*, like a shovel hitting a stone, and decided to follow the clue.

By then Pedersen's crew had been in Igaliku for a few weeks. They'd rented a small white cottage at the top of the village where they slept and cooked and played marathon rounds of Yatzy (the Scandinavian version of Yahtzee) in the evenings. Early each morning they walked down to dig in the Norse cemetery with shovels, picks, and trowels. Most days you could hear them working and talking across town. In Igaliku, archaeology was the loudest thing going on.

The town was the smallest place I would ever visit in the north. Only about twenty people lived there year-round, and the layout was immediately familiar: one store, one church, a pier, and a school, though I believe its students had grown up and moved away—I never saw any children in Igaliku. Out on the water below town three icebergs turned in the current. Often you heard the bleating of sheep. There was one ewe who kept losing her lamb.

Dorthe's team had excavated a pit about the size of a one-car garage. Though it was only a few feet deep they'd found more than thirty skeletons and moved, by hand, twenty tons of earth (Dorthe was the kind to keep meticulous track). The grave soil was dark and damp, and she explained that it wasn't natural: It was Norse-enhanced. Native soil, she explained, was so thin that the Norse had heaped up kitchen scraps, animal bones, bits of wood, and debris to form a kind of funereal mulch that, over time, grew deep enough to accept the dead, though not comfortably. Dorthe's team found them stacked atop each other like planks, like cordwood.

I asked if the team had found any grave goods and they laughed. Nothing: not a scrap of clothing, not a ring or coin. The dead may have traveled onward in thin shrouds of some kind, but none of the material survived.

"They didn't seem to care that much about the mortal remains," Sara told me. "You see it a lot in Europe, too. Just *swoop*—move the bodies aside, make room for the next guy."

The archaeologists' work was part of a long-term population study, which aims, among other things, to know how many Vikings had lived in Greenland during the long colonial period. Over decades, estimates have ranged from a high of about five thousand to today's consensus, which is around twenty-five hundred. Dorthe and her colleagues wanted finer tuning, and they were hoping to get it in cemeteries. From the dead they believed they could reasonably reverse-estimate the size of the living population. This, in turn, could lead them toward a better understanding of population highs and lows, where people concentrated, how many mouths an average farm could feed.

They were also hoping to eventually tease out intersections: Where, for example, a decline in the population might have coincided with a series of harsh winters or dry summers. Or how a decrease in the productivity of farms impacted migration or life expectancy. Or, perhaps, how the bones themselves might reveal the arrival of a disease such as a plague.

Dorthe, who was a paleoepidemiologist by training, wanted trends, directions, even forecasts, in a way, of the past—details that could backfill the enormous holes in our understanding of Norse society. A clearer sense of these things could offer a better glimpse into the colony's obscure inner workings, as well as the challenges its residents faced, especially in the fourteenth and fifteenth centuries, when Greenland grew colder and the colony came undone.

There was, of course, also the Big Question, which loomed over Dorthe's work like a cloud, but also an invitation—a one-of-a-kind riddle that had haunted scholars, explorers, and churchmen for hundreds of years.

"Everyone wants to know what happened to the Norse," she told me.

IN 1721, A FAMILY OF NORWEGIAN MISSIONARIES sailed into Greenland's southern fjords searching for the Norse. They suspected the Norse were still Catholics, or maybe even pagans, and they hoped to convert the settlement to Lutheranism. But the missionaries found only abandoned longhouses and empty byres. The pastures were green but they, too, were empty. Cathedrals still stood, but seemed to have been stripped of ornaments long ago. The missionaries were so unsettled that they refused to believe what the landscape was telling them and for years afterward they kept searching for revenant Vikings.

This for me is one of the most disturbing scenes in the saga, because it suggests that at some point continental Europeans forgot about the Greenlanders. Today archaeologists believe the settlement went dark by 1450, but the last known written records from the colony (a series of letters that mention a wedding twenty-five miles south of Garðar) date to about forty years earlier. It is possible, then, that by the time the missionaries arrived, no one had heard anything from the Norse colony for nearly three hundred years.

This potential gap and the isolation it suggests is astounding. And it means the Norse, for their part, may not have been able to resist their own consignment to oblivion. By the latter days of the colonial period, they don't seem to have had enough wood and iron to build ships worthy of an Atlantic crossing, and so they couldn't leave. Finding passage aboard a visiting ship also may have become impossible because at some point merchants seemed to have stopped traveling to Greenland. In my science-fiction analogy, the Greenlanders become like astronauts stranded on the moon or even the International Space Station. All communication with Europe, all hope of return, may have ceased in the early 1400s. Here the story seems to turn toward tragedy, even horror.

But this is just one way to tell the story, and there have been many.

One of the beautiful and irritating aspects of archaeology is that it allows us to reinterpret the past as often as we like. More discoveries lead to new theories; new technology offers deeper readings. A central tenet that I have always loved about the profession is this: You don't dig up everything. You leave part of any archaeological site untouched, so that future scientists have a chance to do better, with better methods. In terms of the Norse Greenlanders, this approach has allowed the story to change and evolve right up into our own chaotic era.

The oldest theories on Norse collapse, reaching back to the 1700s, held that the Inuit killed them off. Later theories from the 1970s and '80s began to take climate change into account, though it looked opposite to what we're experiencing now. Back then, scholars blamed a period called the Little Ice Age for dooming the Norse. The LIA, as it's often called, was a prolonged period of cold that followed the Medieval Climate Anomaly—that warm spell that had helped the Norse establish themselves in Greenland. Today the LIA is thought to have begun around 1300 and lasted until the mid-1800s. The northern hemisphere cooled slowly at the start; later temperatures fell more rapidly. Eventually, some places cooled by as much as 3.6 degrees Fahrenheit.

To put this in perspective, the 2015 Paris Agreement aimed at limiting climate warming to "well below" a change of 3.6 degrees Fahrenheit. In other words, such a shift is understood to carry potentially significant consequences whether it goes up or down, whether you're talking about cooling or warming. In Europe during the late Middle Ages and into the Renaissance, a drop of this scale was more than enough to create severe problems. Today, the latter phases of the LIA are linked to famine, social unrest, and political upheaval. Some regions saw crops fail and then remain poor for decades, and the strange weather also seems linked to bizarre and tragic human behavior: the end of the LIA coincides with the witch-hunting hysteria that swept Europe and eventually reached North America. The relentless cold (along with starving peasants) may even have helped overturn feudalism and usher in new, market-based economies.

All of that, though, was on the Continent. What did the creeping cold do to the Norse? An archaeologist named Thomas McGovern shared with me a few of the older theories, which tended to focus on Norse overreach. He said, "We used to think, 'Poor dumb Norsemen move to Greenland and bring their cows and when it gets too cold they all die.'"

In the '80s, McGovern was among the researchers who helped build this theory. In it, the Norse were seen as stubborn and conservative, meaning they sailed blithely into a new world and, rather than adapt, tried to force their old way of life onto the fragile landscape. The land responded badly, and when the climate shifted the Norse found they'd destroyed their environment. With no way to get off the island, many, if not most, probably starved.

McGovern told me that more recent scholarship has shown the collapse was probably far more complex. Cold is no longer seen as a driving factor but one in a cascade of problems the Norse faced during the onset of the LIA. And instead of sitting on their hands while their colony ended, it seems the Norse struggled fiercely for survival.

"Now we know that they actually adapted really well," McGovern said. "For a while. But they still died out. So it's a much scarier story."


ON CERTAIN SUNNY DAYS, THE ARCHAEOLOGISTS carry a portable speaker down to the grave pit and listen to pop music, rock 'n' roll, and Inuit rap from Greenland while they attend to the ancient dead. Sometimes they play their theme song, "Excavator," by the YouTube star Blippi, though by the time I meet them the song has been played so much that no one wants to hear Blippi sing about his big bucket anymore. For a while when I'm with them, the team listens to a Danish podcast about unsolved murders.

Sara says, "But we don't have that many murders in Denmark, so there's not too much to talk about."

The dead don't mind. They're coming back up into an age of excess. There is more wood and iron in Igaliku now than these men would've seen in their lifetimes. Better to slide into the present with music and stories. Those, at least, would have been familiar.

For a few days I sit with the team at the grave while they work, asking questions, talking about their theories. While they haven't found any grave goods, they did discover something unusual in the mulch: a piece of a walrus maxilla, a facial bone. Later, when I see it, the bone doesn't look like much—a chunk of plaster, a piece of broken white brick. Dorthe tells me that around the time the grave was in use, there were no walruses this far south, so the bone must have traveled a long way. It's likely it came from Disko or even Melville Bay, which are both hundreds of miles to the north.

In the latest theories of Norse collapse, walruses loom. Many of the scholars I spoke to now believe that the trade in walrus tusks with Europe was not merely a side hustle of an agrarian people but the most important economic activity in the colony. Tusk harvesting may have been even more important than farming. It's possible settlers were drawn to the island specifically because of the tusk trade. Scientists often call it "white gold."

"They are essentially hunters that farm a bit," said Christian Koch Madsen, an archaeologist and deputy director of the Greenland National Museum and Archives in Nuuk. "As opposed to farmers who hunt a little. The white gold seems to have been the thing."

It now appears that for several centuries, the trade was enough to keep ships moving back and forth between Greenland, Iceland, and Europe, hauling tusks away and delivering iron and wood to the Norse. Tusks became a way to ease the material hardships of life on the frontier, but they were never easy to obtain. Each journey north to the hunting grounds, Norðrsetr, was extremely hazardous. Walruses themselves can weigh some two thousand pounds, far more than a polar bear or a musk ox, and they're known as one of the more dangerous Arctic animals because they can so easily overturn small craft.

The hunts would also have been limited by time. Sailing up the coast would likely have been possible only in the summer. Not only would this have stripped farms of laborers during a crucial season, it would have put the futures of entire fjord communities at risk. Imagine just one boat lost with its crew of six or eight men. Such a disaster might've been enough to knock a small farm, or several, into ruin.

The risk compounded as the climate began to cool. A lost boat, a failed crop, fewer walruses: You see the entanglements gathering.

Eventually the tusk trade appears to have collapsed with a push from a different animal: elephants. Elephant ivory had slipped into European markets probably around the time Greenland was settled, but for centuries it was harder to come by. By the late Middle Ages, though, European traders were pushing deeper into Africa and trade networks were expanding. Elephant ivory became easier to get and was considered higher quality. The shift from one tusk to another might have been devastating for the Norse, and it likely led to a decline in ships visiting the island. Fewer ships, of course, meant fewer iron nails, fewer oak timbers. No more immigrants. Maybe no more boats on which to escape.

The image of the Norse as walrus people has quietly shifted our sense not only of their end but also of the Norse themselves. From farmers to hunters, stubborn to flexible, isolated to active in ocean-spanning networks. Even the idea that the Norse might have starved seems to be fading. Chemical analysis of their bones shows that over time their diet shifted from farm products like meat and dairy to a menu of mostly marine mammals, including seals.

Madsen said that what seems to be fairly certain is that the LIA created a more unstable environment, similar to the one we live in now. More than the cold it was the weather that became increasingly unpredictable and problematic. Some experts suggest that with these changes came more sea ice, rising sea levels, drier conditions in the fjords that led to poor harvests of hay.

"It was just all these different things," Madsen said. "Everything's kind of messed up for a while. That's of course not good when you're farming, and you also have to get into small boats and go up north, make these long journeys to get walrus."

Still the Norse adapted, and adapted again. They found food, they traveled ever farther north in pursuit of walruses.

"So, why did they disappear?" Madsen said. "Why, when they were able to feed themselves? That's an even deeper mystery than it used to be."

SHORTLY BEFORE I ARRIVED IN IGALIKU, BIRTE OLSEN made a striking discovery. The first skeleton was an older male. In his arms he held the second, a child of perhaps six years old. The child's body seemed to be turned inward, as though nestling against the man, and the man's arms appeared to be wrapped around the child. Somehow the embrace had outlasted centuries of freezing and thawing, rain, snowmelt, and now warming. It had outlasted the Norse themselves.

When I heard the story I assumed, because nearly all of the skeletons in the grave appeared to be male, that they were father and son. Or at least relatives of some kind.

"Not necessarily," Rikke said. "We think that at the time, if a child died, they would be buried with an older person, a grown-up member of the society."

It meant that the child's parents had likely survived him, and that he'd been buried with a neighbor, or a family friend, or perhaps merely someone who was part of the early Catholic community. In the afterlife, or perhaps on the journey toward it, the older person was supposed to teach the child, guide him in a faith he had been too young to fully comprehend. The adult would ensure that the child did not stray or grow lonely. He would ensure that the child found his way to heaven.

The discovery had touched each of the archaeologists,

these hardened excavators who were used to brushing bones up from the earth. The gesture, whatever it meant to the Norse, appeared to us as a sign of elemental human affection carried into darkness. I had two sons at the time, and the older one was about the same age as the boy from the grave. In any child's death you may glimpse the unspeakable, the unthinkable, and as we talked about the discovery I was suddenly overwhelmed with that rending terror. Somehow the idea of burying a child with a stranger made it worse.

"I think it would have been a more collective society back then," Sara said, seeing my reaction. "We don't think this was unusual for them."

Later Birte shared the archaeological drawings they'd made of the bodies, and Dorthe explained how the bones helped to fill in the details of daily life with braided stories of hardship. The man suffered from severe arthritis and a condition called hypoplasia could be seen in the teeth of the child. This appears when tooth enamel stops growing during times of extreme physiological stress, such as during seasons of starvation.

The child's skull had disintegrated during excavation, but some of his teeth survived. Dorthe held one and pointed out the telltale marks—tiny lines that ran around the tiny tooth. She counted them up. One for every year of his life.

"I think what we're seeing here are the winters," she said. "When things got very, very hard and there wasn't much to eat."

Here was the other side of what Madsen had told me. While the Norse may not have starved to death in the later days of their colony, food was still difficult to come by, especially in winter when the fjords froze and in spring when the ice began to melt and was no longer safe to travel over. The ages of the skeletons tentatively lined up with the start of the LIA—that initial period of cooling. This may have been a time of painful choices, of walrus boats that did not return. Of carefully tended fields failing. In other words, this child may have been born into the beginning of the end.

We sat silently. Birte's eyes were red, their voice gone husky. They admitted they weren't usually moved by bones. This was different.

"It gets you." They laid a hand over their heart. "Right here."

My own eyes burned and I could barely look at the teeth in Dorthe's palm. We all stared away for a few moments into the bright afternoon, toward the icebergs turning in the sea, or the mountains rising over the fjord. From somewhere near the top of town a torrent of bleating let us know the dumb ewe had lost her lamb again.

Later in the evening, after I'd left the team and retreated to my little rented hut, I struggled to not make too much of the man and child. I tried to keep them safely in the past, beyond help or hurt and certainly beyond my ability to know much about them. But some stories can never be neatly corralled, not even very old ones. And a parent's mind is never a rational place. It's a labyrinth of what-ifs and could'ves and nightmares that will probably not come true but that still enjoy a visit, asking for a little of your attention, inviting you to imagine the worst.

I lay awake for a long time thinking of my own sons and this ancient pair, traveling together from the tundra toward some unimaginable destination.

THERE IS A TEMPTATION WHEN CONSIDERING THE lives of ancient people to make them victims, or to absolve them of sins, and to paint our logic, our desires and solutions, over theirs. We remake them into ourselves. We believe they thought like we do, but that they were less capable, or slightly less evolved. We like to replay their stories of struggle and tragedy and imagine we'd escape similar fates. I see this sometimes in my older son. With him it isn't mean or blind; he's too young for that. Instead, it's funny. I tell him of the Greenland Norse and the troubles they faced at the end, and instantly he imagines solutions. *Why didn't they just do this?* he says. *Or eat that? Wanna know what I'd do?*

I love this about his mind—his unlimitedness. I imagine him playing with the little wooden toy, the horse with the braided mane that was found in the midden. He is just past the age where he would've taken it into bed, cradled it in the night like a treasure. None of his solutions would've saved the Norse, but I know he would've kept them good company.

Often enough I see this tendency in myself, too. It's easy to believe we would not fall prey to the same problems or mistakes that ruined the Norse. We are too advanced, we'd say. Our technology is light-years beyond theirs. In those moments I remind myself that the Norse had little agency, little influence on their environment, at least not in the ways we do. They could *respond* to climatic upheaval, they could innovate with driftwood or caribou antler in place of oak planks and iron. But they could not, say, radically reduce their greenhouse emissions, or transition to cleaner energy sources. They couldn't reduce their material consumption or curb their appetite for raw materials. They didn't have these options. We do, though. And we fail again and again to choose them. Here, perhaps, is the great difference between the Norse mind and our own. They tried to survive. Sometimes we don't seem like we want to.

In the end, Greenland was a marginal place. The southern fjords open well below the Arctic Circle, but they have always been extreme, more Arctic than not. The colony, too, was pressed into mere slivers of habitable space between the great glacial ice of the interior and the frigid sea below.

For now there is no evidence of plague, or starvation, or even large-scale exodus or violence. No written records from the era mention disaster. If a large number of Greenlanders managed to get away from the colony as it collapsed, no one seems to have noticed.

I wonder about the stages the Norse passed through, and whether they were similar to others I'd seen in the north. If they truly became a people of the walrus, then the Norse, like the Nunamiut in Anaktuvuk Pass, must have ached as the animals they depended on declined. Maybe they felt their community weaken with the death of each elder—the men and women who'd known the colony's best years, its greatest harvests. At a certain point, too, the

Norse must have reacted like the Tłįchǫ, throwing themselves into action, searching for a way to save the things they loved even when the math or the odds or the outcomes looked grim.

TODAY THE NORSE HAVE NO HEIRS. NO ONE CLAIMS them. This makes their silence and mystery more profound.

I notice it first at grave's edge, where the team has almost no reaction to the bones. There is only the soft sweep of brushes, the *tink tink* of picks and trowels. Some of this is professional detachment, and it isn't always the case—I think of Birte, and their reaction to the discovery of the child. But when I push gently on the notion of ties to the dead, the Danes are quick to dismiss it. "They're just bones," Rikke says one afternoon. "There isn't much connection to whoever they were when they were alive. It's just too long ago."

It's also more than that. Denmark was once a Viking kingdom. It's always considered part of the larger medieval Norse world. The modern nation, too, is thoroughly tied to Greenland through a colonial history that reaches back to the early 1700s. Today the island is a self-governing part of the Danish kingdom. But Danes generally do not think of the Norse Greenlanders as kin. And Greenland, which after the Norse became an entirely Inuit nation, sees itself linked by language, culture, and stories to the Arctic world of the Canadian Inuit and the Iñupiat of Alaska.

Even in Iceland, where many of the original Norse settlers arrived from, there isn't much connection. By way of contrast, many Icelanders are devoted to their lineages. Some can tell you when their families arrived on the island, where exactly they settled. They can trace ancestors back by a medieval manuscript called *Landnámabók*, "The Book of Settlements," that records deeds and details and lives dating back to the arrival of the first settlers in the late ninth century. For Greenland there is no such book.

One day I sat watching Dorthe's team load bones into aluminum boxes for transport back to Copenhagen. I asked Birte if Inuit Greenlanders thought much about the ancient Norse. They smiled.

"No one really cares."

Birte was thirty, and they'd grown up in a generation who wanted independence from Denmark. They nodded at the aluminum crates.

"A few people have said, 'Oh, good for you for getting the Scandinavians out of our country!' But otherwise it's no big deal."

We all laughed. Bones slipped into boxes. Lids clapped shut. Tools were shunted away. In the late-summer sun the boxes gleamed, like fancy luggage. Soon they'd be packed onto a boat and shipped to Nuuk. Then they would travel to Copenhagen.

When I asked Dorthe what the afterlife would look like for these dead, she gave a small laugh and brushed bangs from her eyes.

"In a storage room at the national museum," she said. "Yeah. It sounds bad, I know."

All that trouble, I thought, to gather the grave mulch, to make mounds deep enough, to arrange the bodies and bury them facing east. Only for the dead to wake up at the end of the world in a basement in Copenhagen.

When the packing was done, we grabbed shovels and a wheelbarrow and heaved all twenty tons of ancient grave mulch back into the pit. Later that evening at the crew's cottage, we ate burgers with onions fried in sugar and butter. Then we played Yahtzy with blistered hands. Outside the light was perfect, golden syrup sliding over the fjord and the mountains and Igaliku's little wood houses. Somewhere the ewe was calling for her lamb again. Her voice was the only sound. I asked Dorthe for the last time what she thought had happened to the Norse in this place.

She cast a small tanned hand at the town and said, "I think it looked a lot like this."

The Norse world ended in beauty, then, and silence. The young people gone on boats back to Europe or lost in hunting accidents along the coast. The churches empty, the bishops long dead. No more children's voices in the meadows. Just a few old people hanging on, reluctant to leave homes they'd known all their lives. Maybe it was a door closed softly, Dorthe said. The end of the world doesn't always require catastrophe.

A DAY LATER I LEFT IGALIKU AND HIKED SOUTH DOWN THE SPINE of the peninsula. No one lived anywhere along it and there were no roads, only sheep trails. I went alone and wandered through country the Tuniit would have known, then the Norse, finally the Inuit. For days I saw no one. I hiked past scattered Norse ruins and in one place, now called Sissarlut-toq, came to a small village or farmstead. There, in a notch above the sea, two rivers collided and fell away into a steep ravine. More than a dozen massive Norse structures stood surrounded by old pasture. I could make out a longhouse, its heavy doorway still intact. A byre, perhaps a sheep shed.

I set up my tent on a field of thick grass beside a sheep trail scored so deeply into the earth it reminded me of the paths caribou carved into the Canadian barren lands. The sun set below the mountains and I sat watching with my back pressed to an earthen berm. The last birds flew off. Soon there remained only the noise of the rivers. As the old Norse foundations faded into dusk I thought of the heat required to raise them—you could sense it in the size of the building stones, in the way the walls still held their angles. So much work. Whoever had lived here would never have wanted to leave. In the morning the sun rose over the fjord and its light washed right through the front door of the longhouse, or was it a byre, or some other thing for which we no longer have a name.

I kept walking. One night I camped in the ruins of a cathedral called Hvalsey and I was awoken in the middle of night by a voice—a high fragment of sound, like the last note of a scream. I cowered in my tent for a while, and when I finally crept out I fully expected to find someone there. But the church was empty, the sky spitting rain. I was alone. In the morning I was chopped out of sleep again by another loud sound, and this time I thought it was the church collapsing. But slowly, as my mind cleared, I realized it was a whale, spouting in the fjord below the church.

I relaxed and remembered that Hvalsey, in old Norse, means Whale Island. I gathered myself and crept out of the tent to go watch for the whale, but by the time I reached the shore it had vanished.

While I walked through this wildland of ruins I thought often of the maps Sollie Hugo had shown me in Anakuvuk Pass, rich with names, historical events, and the routes of animals. I wondered if the Norse had mapped the fjords in similar ways, in stories, memories, perhaps even in runes. Did they know what the land held and who had lived there, which animals could be found there and in what season? Surely their long residence in Greenland made them experts.

This mental line led me to a strange question: Did the Norse ever become Indigenous to Greenland, in the way, say, the Tłįchǫ were to their homelands? Even asking this question I know I am stepping close to a hornet's nest. The word *indigenous* is hard to define and carries both a political dimension and a sense of survivorship that the Norse had never known here. In most of our modern conversations, the word has become so charged, so vague, that I do not think most of us really understand what we're talking about when we say it. What *indigenous* communicates now to me, after my journeys through the north, is a sense of belonging that is not manufactured or purchased but earned. A commitment to moral relationships between humans and animals, between humans and land and sea. A respect for the way cold holds everything together. My very loose definition is, I know, so tentative it might describe almost anyone. But still I wonder, how did it apply to the Norse?

Did they ever become more than settlers, did they ever really belong to this part of the north?

Maybe there is no point in asking about an heirless and extinct people. I thought of the Netsilingmiut and the Nunamiut. I thought of their relationships to land and animals, the concepts of belonging held within the word *nuna*. They had walked the tundra and crossed the frozen sea for thousands of years. They had become seal people and caribou people. The Norse had been seal and caribou people, too, though they barely lasted half a millennium in Greenland. What was their equivalent of *nuna* and, perhaps more importantly, *where* was it?

In the end it seemed clear the Norse did not become indigenous here. There are many reasons, but one of them was that they considered themselves part of a larger Norse culture, one rooted in Scandinavian customs and traditions. In Greenland they were Christians, too, tied to the church in Rome. They existed at the outer edges of Continental markets, trade, and desires, but they were still connected to all these things. Whatever struggles they faced in Greenland were not enough to wean them from the old ways. To make them wholly new.

AFTER FOUR DAYS OF HIKING I RETURNED TO IGALIKU and made my way north to Nuuk. There I would argue collegially about Norse identity with Christian Madsen. He disagreed with me. He believed the Norse had indeed become indigenous to Greenland and his defense made sense. It almost convinced me.

He had just returned from fieldwork high in the mountains where he and some colleagues had located a caribou hunting site that was apparently used by Inuit and Norse at around the same time. It was a stunning discovery, made on open ground just below the inland ice sheet—a remote area where no one had ever thought to look. Madsen said the site appeared to show that the Norse had at least the same depth of knowledge about caribou behavior as the Inuit. And he reminded me that the Norse had arrived in Greenland earlier.

What has stuck in my mind since my talk with Madsen and my long walk through the country is that the Norse did not necessarily need to go extinct, or abandon their homes and return to Europe. When the world changed around them they had another option, but they apparently refused to take it.

By the end of the colonial period in the mid-1400s, the Inuit (sometimes called the Thule) had moved into the southern fjords. They lived in many of the same regions the Norse did, sometimes just outside Norse settlements. When the LIA intensified, when the weather grew more unpredictable and the seas more dangerous, the Norse tried almost everything they could to adapt. They ate more marine mammals. They wore clothing made of caribou skin. They hunted and perhaps in some way even worshipped the walrus. They became, in other words, a lot more like their new Inuit neighbors.

But there seemed to be a line they would not cross: They refused to fully become Arctic nomads, like the Inuit, even when it might have allowed them to stay, or to survive.

Scholars told me the Norse might not have recognized this as a real choice. Their identity was tethered to the old world—a cord too thick for cutting. Perhaps all we can say of them now is that when their environment demanded changes, they were willing to go along, up to a point.

It's still possible, of course, that we simply haven't yet found evidence of more extensive Norse adaptions. Maybe it's out there, somewhere, waiting to be discovered, like the women and children missing from the cemetery at Garðar. It occurs to me now, a couple of years later, that we are doing no better than the Norse at adapting to our own transforming world, and possibly we're doing much worse. Like them, we face a cascade of threats. Almost certainly we'll need to become something new to meet them.

ONE AFTERNOON I HAD COFFEE WITH A GREENLANDIC archaeologist named Kirstine Eiby Møller. We met in a café near the harbor, under a sky busy with cranes. Nuuk was experiencing a building boom, driven in part by interest in the wealth of untapped minerals Greenland is believed to possess. Down at the water, huge cruise ships were coming and going. Soon direct flights between Nuuk and New York City would begin. In some areas the feeling of a gold rush was gathering. I thought of the Norse and the white gold, the walrus tusks, that had led many of them here a thousand years before.

Møller worked at the Greenland National Museum and Archives, and when we were done with our coffee she suggested we go there. The museum was closed, but she had a key. She said that I had spent so much time with the Norse that she wanted me to see the other part of the story.

Inside, the museum was dark and quiet. We cruised past the exhibits, our reflections flitting over glass cases of clothing, weapons, tools. At the back of one gallery, she led me to the door of a small room that stood off the main hall. Møller explained that the room was offset on purpose because what was inside had such affecting potential. In other words, visitors had to make a conscious decision about whether or not to enter.

"I hate it when museums don't give you a choice," she said. "I don't like going into a museum and being forced to see, like, the Egyptian mummies."

I'd never thought about it that way. Standing now before the dark threshold, it seemed obvious. Necessary.

Møller had brought me to see the so-called Qilakit-soq mummies, which are the naturally preserved bodies of eight Inuit who died around the late middle of the fifteenth century. The bodies were discovered in 1972 near a now-abandoned town called Qilakitsoq, which lies far above the Arctic Circle. The dead had been buried under rocks and preserved unintentionally by the cold dry air. After archaeologists retrieved them, four were sent to Copenhagen, where they remain in storage; the others were put on display in Nuuk. They included three adult women and one infant, thought to be about six months old at the time of death. Before we went in, Møller warned me, one parent to another, "You see them differently when you have children."

The room was small and dim, the walls and ceiling black. Behind a pane of glass the mummies lay atop caribou skins in the positions in which they'd been buried. The women's legs were gently bent at the knees. The baby, believed to be a boy, had been laid against the right hip of one of the women. She may have been his mother. All were dressed in fine clothing of caribou and seal skins. The women wore tall, intricately sewn boots. The boy wore leggings and a parka, and the tiny hood had been pulled up over his head.

I remember stepping back. In the boy I saw my sons.

"You see," Møller said at my shoulder. "I told you."

The mummies' skin, though shriveled and tight to the bone, was intact. So was their hair, their teeth. The eye sockets were black and empty. The women's faces still bore the faint lines of tattoos. The baby's eyebrows were slightly arched, his tiny lips almost pursed. His eyelashes, the tiny crumpled hands, were all perfect. When you came near, he seemed to gaze expectantly up into your face, as though he were hoping to nurse.

Møller explained that no one knew what happened to these people, only that they had died around the same time. It had been autumn, perhaps 1460 or 1475. The dates lined up closely with the final collapse of the Norse colony, some seven hundred miles away to the south.

"This is the other part of the story," Møller said. "These people died at the same time, and yet their culture lived on. People buried them. We know the Inuit lived."

She might have said, *I know because I am one.*

Møller had a five-year-old daughter. She had seen the mummies many times and was always moved, though it bothered her that they were on display. Many Greenlanders felt that way, she said. Many people believed they should be returned to their resting place and left in peace. I recalled that no one worried like this for the Norse dead.

It is believed that the baby may have been buried alive, beside his dead mother. This was just a theory, based on the fact that nothing appeared to be wrong with him, and that Inuit oral histories suggest the practice was not unheard of. The logic, so far as we understand it, held that a mother-less child at such a young age would have no one to care for him, no one to nurse him. In the harsh Arctic environ-ment, it was thought better for everyone, perhaps, to send the baby onward into the next life with his mother.

Møller and I stood for a while in silence, looking at the child, thinking of our own. I thought too of the Norse boy Birte Olsen had found, the one curled into the arms of a stranger.

My eyes began to sting. Somewhere in the museum we heard voices, laughter. A private tour was coming through. We headed back outside and walked into town where Møller's daughter waited for her at a café, eating french fries with her grandfather. We hugged and said goodbye. She returned to her life, and I headed onward, toward my rented room by the sea. It was almost September. In the evening a little snow would fall.

Somewhere out there the world was ending.

# BORDERLANDS

*Kirkenes, Norway*

W E ARE WAITING FOR ANOTHER GORBACHEV,"
Georgii Chentemirov said. "A reformer. Someone inside."

"What do you mean?" I said.

The Russian smiled and set down his cup. In the small
lunch room there was a scent of singed coffee and spilled
sugar glinting on a table. Pale light filtered through a window. "People in the West think Navalny will come out of
prison and suddenly everything will change."

Chentemirov was talking about Alexei Navalny, the
Moscow lawyer and opposition leader who'd been jailed in
2021 and who would be dead in early 2024.

"Change will never happen like that in Russia," Chentemirov said. "There's too much system. It will not be that
kind of revolution."

We were sitting in the office of *The Barents Observer*, a
small newspaper based in Kirkenes, a town in Arctic Norway just six miles west of the Russian border. Beside us

on the floor stood a large framed portrait of Mikhail Gorbachev. In the photo he looked young, hopeful. As though
he were enjoying Chentemirov's commentary.

"We need someone from inside the system." Chentemirov nodded toward Gorbachev. "*He* was inside the
system. That's why he changed things. Though maybe not
like he wanted."

Chentemirov was a reporter, and he'd worked at the
*Observer* for less than a year. Before that he'd written for a
newspaper back home, in the Russian republic of Karelia,
where he'd also been president of the journalists' union.
But that life already seemed far away. Now Chentemirov
lived in exile with his family in Kirkenes, and he wrote
stories in Russian for the *Observer*. The paper, which was
banned in Russia, then beamed his stories over the border,
past censors, using a variety of apps, social media platforms, and mirror sites. Every story Chentemirov wrote
seemed to separate him a little more from home. He told
me he wasn't sure he'd ever return.

"Probably not unless something really big changes," he
said, sighing. In a sign of acceptance, or maybe submission,
he'd started studying to get a Norwegian driver's license.
The test was coming up. Chentemirov was a funny guy, always cracking jokes, making his colleagues laugh, but the
Norwegian driver's manual had actually made *him* laugh.

"So many rules here," he said. "It's crazy."

WHEN I MET HIM, CHENTEMIROV WAS ONE OF FOUR
new reporters the *Observer* had hired—three Russians and

one Ukrainian—in what was described to me as a battle against evil. This was how the editor of the paper, Thomas Nilsen, sometimes talked. A lot of his American contemporaries would've balked at such candor and muttered something about bias, about balance, about provocative language. Nilsen, though, felt he'd earned his perspective. He'd been living next door to Russia and reporting on the country for more than twenty years. He was old enough to remember the Cold War well, and he'd even lived inside Russia for a while after the collapse of the USSR. By the time Vladimir Putin rose to power and began to hoard it, Nilsen was what you might call a *subject matter expert*: He was the kind of journalist other journalists called when they wanted to know what Russia was up to in the far north.

The *Observer* was a purely digital paper run by Nilsen and his colleague Atle Staalesen, and it was dedicated to covering the Arctic—the entire Arctic. Special attention was given to Russia and stories affecting the borderland with Norway, but the men aimed at an international audience, and for two decades they'd been publishing in English and Russian. They didn't even bother with Norwegian, since most of their fellow citizens spoke English anyway.

Their mission was ambitious, even if it was enormous, and I'd been reading the *Observer* for years before I visited. I appreciated the way Nilsen and Staalesen opened up parts of the Arctic that the American media rarely noticed. Before the invasion of Ukraine, the pair had essentially done everything themselves. Nilsen was the editor and Staalesen was the publisher. Both men reported stories, wrote editorials, scanned the wires. They did the back-office stuff, too, like answering phones, dealing with unhappy politicians (usually Russian), and paying bills.

As a former news reporter myself, there was something else I liked about the *Observer*. They were a paper for the world, but they still felt embedded in an actual place, like a small-town local. Nilsen told me that once, before Ukraine, before the *Observer* had been banned in Russia, and before he himself had been declared a persona non grata there and hauled off a bus at the border, he and Staalesen used to drive into the country and work there. They'd do interviews, take photos, roam around. Russians even used to call the office with news tips.

Those were the good old days, and now they seemed impossibly distant, almost like a folk story. Ukraine had changed everything, and in the aftermath, Nilsen was more certain than ever that he was watching the nation next door descend into a kind of ultraviolent psychosis, driven by Putin himself. Nilsen told me that he was still fond of Russians generally, but Putin? If you couldn't use the word *evil* to describe him, what good was the word at all?

"We said, 'Okay, if Putin is escalating his anti-democratic developments, we will also escalate,'" Nilsen had told me on the phone before I arrived. "So we opened the doors for Russian journalists who have fled. Now we've become quite a powerful newsroom. Just look, our staff has grown by 250 percent! We're *The New York Times* of the Arctic."

BACK IN THE LUNCH ROOM, CHENTEMIROV WAS ABOUT to tell me why he'd gone into exile—the story involved something called "the list"—when Nilsen stuck his head in the door.

"Ready?" he said.

Chentemirov stood and gave a mock salute to Gorbachev and we all headed downstairs.

Nilsen had buzzed graying hair, while Chentemirov's was longer and blond. Both men were very tall, the tallest reporters I'd ever met. But they still folded neatly into Nilsen's red Tesla. I climbed in back, feeling a little like luggage.

"Man, I can't wait to drive this thing," Chentemirov said.

"You'll like it," Nilsen said.

"Where are we going?" I asked.

Nilsen smiled. "To the most controversial place in the Arctic."

It seemed suddenly strange that my journey through the north was ending like this. Not on a remote patch of ice, or in winter darkness, or among wild animals or hunters, but in an electric car with a couple of other journalists.

Nilsen jabbed the pedal and the car jumped forward without a sound.

I NEVER WANTED TO WRITE ABOUT BORDERS, I WANTED to cross them. Once I'd even dreamed of entering Russia and continuing east across the Arctic all the way to the Chukchi Sea, but that idea began to crumble in 2014, when Russia illegally annexed Crimea, and then it became impossible after the invasion of Ukraine. Now even this remote corner of Norway, hundreds of miles from the front line,

seemed to crackle with strange potential. I had never encountered an artificial division of this kind anywhere else
in the far north. And against the mythic scale of everything
else I was trying to know, the sudden appearance of such a
barrier seemed more than unnatural. It was cruel. I would
learn that not even reindeer were allowed to freely cross.

The borders that mattered, I had thought, were not
imaginary lines drawn between nation-states that might
not survive another century. What mattered were shifting
edges of ice and water, earth and stone, trees, light, darkness. Language. The movement of animals.

I thought, for instance, of how a traveler could begin
in Greenland and travel west through Canada to Alaska
and never really leave the shared culture of the Inuit and
the Iñupiat. You could—and some explorers had done
it—cross the sweep of Arctic North America listening to
variations of the same ancient stories told in dialects of the
same ancient tongue. I thought too about the boundaries
that defined caribou lives: the tree line, the snow line, seis-
mic lines and lines of frost, roads, paths of wind and rivers,
even their own trails etched deeply into the tundra. And I
thought of the routes of whales and wolves, who accept no
limitations on their wandering and routinely remind us of
this by showing up where we least expect them.

Compared to any of these things, the scratches we add
to maps seem less certain than sandcastles, and writing
anything about them felt as though it also could not last. I
wanted to ignore the border between Norway and Russia,
but I couldn't. By the time I reached it, the border seemed
to be the only thing anyone could see.

I ARRIVED IN KIRKENES IN EARLY MAY, ON A COLD gray day shortly before the sun became the midnight sun, when it stayed up around the clock. While the plane circled for its approach, Russian soldiers just over the border may or may not have been jamming its GPS. It wasn't the kind of thing pilots talked about, but the Russians had been doing it, on and off, for a while. Later, when I asked Nilsen why they did it, he shrugged. In his work he had amassed a catalog of such behavior, things Russia did that seemed designed partly to test how Norway would respond, and partly to say, *Fuck you guys*. Nilsen said, "Why do they do anything? Because they can. Because they like to mess with us. Show us who's boss."

The border, then, as a dare. A taunt. A provocation.

On the way into town, I was surprised, though I shouldn't have been, to find thick stands of birch. Kirkenes sits about two hundred and fifty miles above the Arctic Circle, but the fading tendrils of the Gulf Stream and the North Atlantic current push warm water and air up into the region, making it far lusher than, say, Gjoa Haven in Arctic Canada, at about the same latitude.

At an intersection I saw a small herd of reindeer, the slightly smaller cousins of caribou. They were grazing on a median. In Europe, and especially in Norway, Finland, and eastern Russia, caribou are allowed to wander, though they are not so much free-ranging as semidomesticated, an *almost* wild animal often kept as livestock by an Indigenous group called the Sami. As we passed, a few were stepping out into traffic.

I rolled down the window, heard the hollow clatter of

their hooves against pavement. Here, instead of rivers, they crossed roads. I understood that no matter where I'd previously been, I had never seen an Arctic like this.

KIRKENES HAD ONCE BEEN A MINING TOWN. IT WAS built beside an iron-ore deposit on a peninsula in a fjord called Bøkfjorden. For nearly a century, beginning in the early 1900s, the town and its several thousand residents were *ore* people, their fates tied to rock. After the mine closed in the late 1990s, Kirkenes was forced to reinvent itself, and it did, sort of, by turning toward the other feature that defined the area: the border.

Russians had begun driving over into Norway just a few years after the collapse of the Soviet Union. They entered at a place called Storskog, which lies about fifteen minutes by car east of the town center. In the 2000s, cross-border traffic picked up as Russia's economy recovered, and soon Russians were coming to buy vegetables, dishwasher pods, disposable diapers, and other things that were hard to find in the grocery stores back home.

Norwegians too drove through Storskog to Russia, where they bought vodka and cheap gasoline, stopped at cafés in formerly exotic and opaque Russian towns like Nikel, or even the city of Murmansk. Youth hockey leagues held cross-border tournaments. Scientists were able to collaborate with their foreign peers on problems of industrial pollution. Cross-border marriages were, if not exactly common, also not unusual. Nilsen had been able to drive over to do journalism, and he could even drink beer in bars frequented by the Russian military. Once, he told me, some soldiers bought him a drink and raised theirs in greeting.

At peak neighborliness, in 2013, there were 320,000 border crossings, and this, if nothing else, showed how easy it was to come and go from a country that, during my childhood in the 1980s and early '90s, had been shut away behind the Iron Curtain.

Then, in what seems in hindsight like a sequence of swift blows, Russia invaded and annexed Crimea in 2014, the Covid-19 pandemic shut down and reshaped the world in 2020, and Russian troops poured into Ukraine in 2022. Years separated these events, but at the border they seemed to congeal and grow into something like a change in climate, a political cooling trend that slowly built into an ice age.

By the time I visited Kirkenes, Arctic border traffic had been hammered by sanctions against the Russian economy, by pandemic-era restrictions, and then by Norwegian border tightening. This last move came as a kind of soft punishment for Russia's stunning violence against Ukraine. The border was still open—Norwegians couldn't quite bring themselves to shut it completely—but the coming and going had thinned to a trickle.

Russians could still get through but needed a visa, and those were harder and harder to come by. Norwegians, for their part, seemed mostly to lose interest in visiting the bully next door. The border had stopped being fun or lucrative or easy. It had hardened, knuckled into itself. It now did quite plainly what borders always force you to do, which is to pick a side, whether you want to or not.

SUCH WAS THE STATE OF AFFAIRS WHEN I RODE WITH
the two reporters from the *Observer* toward the most controversial place in the Arctic. Nilsen took the long way
to give me a little tour. Downtown Kirkenes might have
been declining, and you could sense a kind of psychic film
growing over the storefronts, like an eye going milky, but
there remained a comfortable middle-class prosperity. It
felt visually familiar, like certain American suburbs.

Neat houses, clean streets, a movie theater, a couple of
bakeries, a bar, and a few restaurants. At the top of town
there was a small mall with a food court; below that was a
shipyard where Russian trawlers docked for repairs. And
on the other side of town there was a passenger-ship termi-
nal. Street signs were in English, Russian, and Norwegian.
Anyone with a car could drive to Oslo, Paris, or Rome.
The most surprising thing I saw on our short trip were
Nazi bunkers. Kirkenes had been occupied for four years
during the war, and the Germans, using prisoners and slave
labor, had gone all-in on military infrastructure.

Much of the German stuff, along with nearly all of
Kirkenes itself, had been obliterated by Allied bombing
raids. But some old concrete buildings had been repur-
posed into garages, sheds, even a house. I had never really
known just how far north the Nazis carried their grim
fantasy. Nilsen stopped the car at a small park outside the
center of town. We got out and he said there was an air-raid
shelter carved into the rock beneath our feet. It was large
enough for more than two thousand people.

At the center of the park, on a tall stone plinth, stood
a large bronze statue of a World War II–era Soviet soldier.

He was heroic, larger than life, with a fine jaw and bulging thighs. He carried a submachine gun and gazed gravely toward the horizon where, you were meant to understand, he was watching for Nazis. At the base of the plinth several bouquets of flowers were arranged. Beside them stood larger, almost funereal displays of plastic flowers in the red, yellow, and blue of the Russian flag.

It was May 9, the day Russians celebrate their victory over the Germans in what they call the Great Patriotic War. Earlier, a small crowd of Russians had gathered at the statue to lay the bouquets and arrange the plastic and celebrate the liberation of Kirkenes, which the Red Army had accomplished in October 1944. Normally the celebration was a joint affair, attended by Russians and large numbers of Norwegians. Even many decades later, the Norwegians were still grateful to the Soviets (and their inheritors, the Russians) not only for liberation but for what the Red Army had done *after* chasing the Germans away: They went home.

That is, they occupied Arctic Norway only briefly. They did not try to seize Kirkenes or roll the north of Norway into the postwar Soviet empire. And this was sort of incredible. In Kirkenes people still spoke about it with quiet awe, as though it were tentative, a stroke of luck that might yet be undone.

The invasion of Ukraine had killed the notion of shared celebration, however. At that morning's memorial service, there was perhaps one Norwegian present, not counting Nilsen, who'd attended as a reporter. At a certain point he'd walked up to the Russian consul, a small owlish man named Nikolai, and tried to interview him about the irony of it all.

"How is it, Nikolai," he had said in a video of the encounter, "to be here on this day of liberation when your country is attacking another neighboring country in Europe?"

The consul wore wire-frame glasses and had a large ribbon on his chest. Behind him a couple of old Russian women clutched bundles of carnations and looked worried. Probably they'd driven over the border for the memorial, and here was a reporter, gumming it up. In Russia, you got arrested for that sort of thing.

Nikolai, however, was calm, cool. Apparently he never answered questions about Ukraine. He merely glanced from side to side, as though the looming Norwegian had not spoken, as though he was not there. After a few moments he went back to celebrating the glorious past.

The whole encounter summed up quite neatly the state of affairs between the neighboring nations, but I still didn't know what we were doing below the statue.

Nilsen said, "Now we wait for the object."

EARLY IN HIS JOURNALISM CAREER, NILSEN HAD worked at a radio station in the Pasvik valley, not far south from Kirkenes. It was technically a news station, but it also played a lot of pop music, and this was broadcasted up through the trees with a big transmitter that stood about a thousand feet from what was then the border with the Soviet Union.

It was 1990, and in between sets of Sinéad O'Connor and the Scorpions, Nilsen and his colleagues read news of the world. At some point they realized Russians were tuning in—for the pop, not the news—and they decided to speak more directly to their neighbors. They brought in a translator and started producing stories in Russian. It was strange to imagine Russian miners or nickel smelters across the valley suddenly getting Western-style news in their own language. Nilsen always wondered if they tuned out or turned it up.

At the time the USSR was hemorrhaging. Surely the Russians across the Pasvik River felt a shift in the ground, in the air. Maybe listening to the radio they caught a headline about demonstrations in the Baltics or riots in the Caucasus. Maybe it helped them understand the tremors all around them. If the local apparatchiks ever noticed the pirate-radio reports, they didn't seem to care.

Then, in 1991, KGB agents and Soviet troops started shooting pro-democracy protesters in Vilnius. Nilsen and his crew translated the news as quickly as they could. He told me they were able to broadcast it for a couple of hours before the Soviets jammed the station's signal. Several months later Lithuania wrenched itself free of Soviet control, and by the end of the year the USSR itself had collapsed. Nilsen never knew how many Russians actually heard the Vilnius broadcasts. He liked to think they'd played a tiny role in the fall of the empire next door, though this, too, was unknowable. Ripples on the sea, a stone thrown into a well. Probably they had no effect at all. The Arctic was a long way from Moscow.

But the small act made Nilsen proud. He went on to do other things—he worked, for instance, with a nuclear non-proliferation group that helped clean up derelict Soviet submarines—but the radio job shaped his career, grounded his faith in a free press. It had shown him how porous borders could be. Eventually Nilsen returned to journalism and after the invasion of Ukraine he immediately knew that he wanted to do that kind of thing again—stand up to the Bear, to the bully. Shine a light into the darkness. I was envious. Very few things in my journalism career had ever felt that purposeful.

"In many ways I feel like I've been a passenger on a thirty-year circle that has come back to where it was," he said. "The Iron Curtain is back, and now it is worse."

The important thing was to keep moving, keep pushing, Nilsen told me. Otherwise all was lost.

MANY NORWEGIANS FELT SIMILARLY, UP TO A POINT. I'd see plenty of Ukrainian flags hanging in the windows during my stay. But when it came to action? As a people, as a culture, the Norwegians were not given to loud displays of outrage, at least not along the Arctic border. They also knew that no matter what they did, they were stuck with the Bear. It was like the midnight sun, the polar night, the cold, the ice: There was not much to do but endure it. The Bear was simply too big for anything else.

Not everyone agreed. Some Ukrainians lived in Kirkenes and the towns around it, and there were a few Norwegians who were willing to loudly denounce Russian violence. Simmering resentments had recently focused here, on the statue commemorating the Soviet liberators. And when those tensions blew up, it usually took the form of flowers.

Supporters of Ukraine dropped bouquets in yellow-and-blue, or they strung little plastic Ukrainian flags on the shrubs around the bronze soldier. Russians would follow and tear down the decorations and sometimes hang their own. That morning, before the memorial service, Nilsen told me a squad of Russian men had scoured the park, pulling up anything Ukrainian. Chentemirov, who was poking around along the edges of the park, had just found a bunch of Ukraine flags stuffed in a trash can. The whole thing felt ridiculous, but also vaguely sinister, like a warm up to something worse. We hadn't been talking for ten minutes when a dark car pulled up and two stocky men got out.

"Here is the object," Nilsen said.

One of the men walked over and while Nilsen and Chentemirov began recording interviews with him, I wrote the man's name down in my notebook. He was Mykhailo Kozachenko, a Ukrainian who'd lived in Kirkenes for thirteen years. He carried a sign and a nylon Ukrainian flag. He draped the flag over the Russian flowers and hung the sign on the plinth, midway between the ground and the bronze soldier's bulging thighs.

On the sign was a portrait of Oleksandr Matsievskyi, a Ukrainian soldier whose execution by the Russians early in the invasion had been filmed and then posted to the web. Matsievskyi had instantly become a martyr, for in the gruesome video, seconds before he is shot, he can be heard saying, "*Slava Ukraini*"—glory to Ukraine.

Matsievskyi's portrait had been hanging here earlier that day. It was one of the decorations the Russians had cleared out. This was an identical copy, and Kozachenko placed it perfectly on the statue. Now the first thing any visitor to the Soviet soldier would see was a Ukrainian one.

"This is a real hero," Kozachenko said.

Nilsen leaned over and whispered, "That sign will not be there in the morning."

In fact it would not last to the end of the day.

We headed back to the Tesla. Nilsen planned to post the video he'd made to the *Observer*'s Instagram and Facebook accounts, and he'd have it translated into Russian and shared over Telegram. Using all three, he explained, there was a better chance it would get around Russian censors and actually reach Russian people.

Before we left, I noticed a small line of text running below the portrait of the martyred Ukrainian. It said, in English, "Russia make no mistake about it; you are the Nazis now."

THE INVISIBLE LINE THAT SEPARATES NORWAY FROM Russia begins in a clearing in dense forest about two hundred miles above the Arctic Circle. A sturdy little tower of rocks marks the spot, and in Norwegian it is called Treriksrøysa, or three-country cairn, because Finland's border meets the others here, too. It's a quiet spot. There isn't a lot to see and there aren't many visitors for such an unusual confluence of states. This is perhaps because Treriksrøysa can't be reached from Finland or Russia, both of which forbid their citizens and anyone else from approaching the borderland. To get there, you must drive through one of the most lightly populated regions of Norway, park your car in a little lot, and hike.

At Treriksrøysa itself there is no watchtower and rarely ever a border guard, though signs in several languages warn that while walking into Finland is okay, crossing into Russia is very much not. The signs also let you know, in case you were wondering, that you're perpetually under surveillance, probably by all three countries.

Heading north, you leave Finland behind and follow the border between Norway and Russia, which runs for some hundred and twenty miles before it vanishes into the Barents Sea. Along almost the entire length, on the Norwegian side, stand a series of posts about four feet high. They appear at regular intervals and are decorated like goldfinches, with black caps and bright yellow bodies. Each is matched on the Russian side by a post painted red and green—a peppermint candy. Together they mark the frontier, though not the border itself, which runs invisibly between them, through forests, over hills, across old battlefields, and sometimes along the bottom of a river.

It occurred to me that the posts marked off a kind of extremely truncated *hozi de*—that transitional zone of the barren lands named by the Tłı̨chǫ. In those places where a river forms the border, international law holds that the actual borderline runs down the middle of the deepest part of the river channel, no matter where it is. Spring floods and winter freezing can, of course, alter the channel, and this means that under the water, unseen by all humans, the border is forever shifting, moving, eroding, and being remade. Spring salmon running over this line became subjects of Russia or Norway with flicks of their tails. Birds glided over it and noticed nothing. That the river itself flowed and flooded and refused to obey, constantly unmaking and remaking the border, was the only true thing I could find. Everything else was performance.

In late 2015, the Russian government began a brief experiment along the border that seemed to illustrate this idea: it allowed refugees and asylum seekers to pour out of Russia and over the Norwegian border. These people had previously entered Russia from all over, but many were Syrians who'd escaped the civil war in their own country and ended up in southern Russian towns. Some had lived in Russia for several years. Some had work visas or student visas. But the economy had changed, jobs were harder to find, and the country had become less welcoming to foreigners. Some—including Thomas Nilsen—suspected there was a strategy behind the flood: weaponized migration designed to destabilize the Arctic.

That year Europe as a whole struggled with unprecedented waves of immigration from Syria, Africa, and beyond, and Russia was not alone—many southern nations cooled to the new arrivals, and some tried to actively prevent them from entering or staying. The Arctic border had never been very involved in the crisis; it was cold and remote. But that year, in autumn, the number of border crossers exploded—two hundred in early October, six hundred in one week later that month. Then the arrivals began to swell. People came in waves by bus. By the end of the year more than five thousand people had arrived in Kirkenes, almost double the number who lived there.

The sudden influx nearly overwhelmed the town. But residents rallied and opened a shelter. People brought food, blankets, and other supplies. At the border itself tents were set up, because winter was near and temperatures were quickly falling. Many of the refugees became asylum seekers. Some were sent south toward Oslo. Then the flood stopped.

Nilsen had been there, reporting on it all. He told me the flood appeared to have been a test, designed to see what Norway would do, what its capabilities were. In other words, Norway had been used as a laboratory. Later Russia would run a similar kind of operation against Finland. The Finns accused Russia of "hybrid warfare" and eventually closed their border with Russia. The Norwegians, despite everything, did not.

I asked Nilsen if he was being too harsh on the Russians. Almost every country in Europe had struggled to deal with mass movements of human beings that year, and many of them had responded cruelly. He raised an eyebrow, and then he told me this story. Once, when he'd been at the border reporting on the migrant crisis, he observed a man standing near the crossing, unloading bicycles from the trunk of a car. The man appeared to be an FSB officer, and migrants told Nilsen that he was selling bikes for $200 apiece. People bought them and struggled over the border, slipping in the ice and snow. Some barely knew how to ride and came careening into Norway. But there was no other way to do it—they weren't allowed to walk, they weren't allowed to hitchhike. As soon as they got across the migrants ditched the bikes. Later I learned the Norwegian government destroyed or recycled most of them after they were deemed unsafe.

DURING THE FEW WEEKS I SPENT IN THE REGION, I was able to drive or walk along much of the border, following the yellow posts through sublime, spring-sodden country. On the Norwegian side, it was easy: You could go virtually anywhere you wanted.

On a warm Saturday I drove the road that followed the border all the way to the end of Europe. During the drive I'd passed cabins and campsites, RVs parked in meadows, an old stone church and a pair of pit houses from the days of nomadic hunters, six thousand years ago. Here and there Norwegian families were out enjoying themselves. Scents of barbecue drifted along the border, and some Boy Scout–looking kids fired pellet guns at paper targets in the grass by the sea.

One tourist I met had driven his camper all the way up from Switzerland. He came to watch seabirds, to gaze out toward the North Pole. He sat in the sun outside his well-appointed van, drinking a beer. He told me he'd been trying to avoid the news. More than a thousand miles south, Russian troops were crawling over Ukraine, and Russian missiles were blowing its cities to dust.

I walked along the frontier for hours that day. Even

way out here the Nazis had been busy, and above the coast I found more of their ruins, bunkers and gun emplacements and bits of twisted steel that jutted from the dunes like ugly fossils. At one spot not far from the bunkers stood a giant cross. It loomed there, in defiance of wind and sun, and it had probably been raised years ago in defiance of the communists. When I looked east into Russia, that era was as hard to imagine as the distant destruction in Ukraine. There was no suggestion of the gulag or the Communist Party, of pograms or perestroika or anything else from that time. There was nothing to see but miles of empty country. Over there Russia looked just like Norway, only lifeless.

AT CERTAIN POINTS ALONG THE BORDER, THE NORWEGIAN military maintains observation posts. Most are small, like backcountry cabins, with room for a few soldiers. The outposts tend to be remote; to reach them you often must hike or drive in some kind of all-terrain vehicle or snowmobile. But they're also well-appointed, even cozy, with woodstoves, kitchens, TVs, well-stocked bookshelves, and video game consoles. The whole system is exceedingly civilized. It's also run by conscripts, soldiers so young they are barely out of high school.

When I visited the largest of these outposts, a sauna was under construction near the gym. Just off the entrance was a collection of artifacts soldiers had discovered over years of patrolling in the hills. They included gray-black Nazi helmets, shattered green Soviet ones, pieces of knives, grenades, mortar shells. I couldn't help arranging these ob-

jects in my mind, holding them up against things I'd found
or seen elsewhere in the north. Arrowheads with the Tłįchǫ.
The gift of the hide scraper from Clyde Morry in Anaktuvuk Pass. The little Norse horse found in an ancient trash
heap in Greenland. So often we think of the earth as swal-
lowing our relics, our bodies. In the Arctic I always found
the ground was trying to give them back.

I spent a couple of long days with the soldiers in various places. I hiked up to the top of a mountain overlooking the sea with them and watched a Russian coast guard
ship nose up to the border. And I visited other outposts
farther south, in high open country that was still mired
in snow. To me the conscripts looked like kids, though of
course they were not kids at all. They'd been entrusted by
their government with one of its most sensitive domestic
missions. They spent their days watching Russia through
enormous telescopes. They were technically the first line
of defense against the Bear.

Really, though, none of the soldiers I met spent much
time worrying about that. Russia had such an advantage
in terms of troops, equipment, and air power that I was
told Norway didn't bother to fortify or mine or even fence
its border. Nor were its outposts heavily garrisoned. There
were never more than half a dozen soldiers in any of the
outposts I saw, and they all said the same thing: We watch
Russia. We make sure tourists don't do anything stupid.
Sometimes we have to deal with reindeer.

At the big outpost, called Korpfjell, a twenty-year-old
soldier named Sondre Aarli took me up into the observation
tower and together we stood outside on a deck, scanning

the stunning landscape below. Deep in the trees a thread of silver was the Jakobselv, Jacob's River, which flowed north to the sea. Forests, lakes, and low mountains spread away on all sides. In Russia, I could see old towers, the kind you'd find keeping watch over a prison. In Norway, I noticed a length of plastic mesh fence. It looked hardly sturdy enough to stop anyone. I pointed it out to Aarli and he said, "For reindeer."

After a while of silence he said, "So, what do you think?"

It was his way of asking, not unkindly, if I had seen enough. If he could get back to the mission, keeping an eye on the forest, the reindeer, the Russians. I was reluctant to leave. The sun was warm, the view expansive. An illusion of timelessness lay on the land like a drug. Some places you know you'll never see again, and I felt my northern journey ending.

We climbed down from the tower. There were waffles waiting in the dining room. We ate them with jam and milk and a sweet brown cheese. I asked the soldiers around the table about the war in Ukraine and how it had affected their lives. They all insisted nothing had changed. They felt no danger. Patrols had not increased. There were no more soldiers stationed along the border than there had been before. Norway had done nothing, in other words, to change its posture along the border.

A couple of days earlier a senior officer had told me, "We want to be predictable."

This, as far as I could tell, was Norway's entire border policy. But as the war grew worse in Ukraine, one year bleeding into another, with civilian deaths rising, cities collapsing, the Russians relentlessly poking and prodding, I wondered how far the good-neighbor routine could go. I never truly understood why the Russians were doing the things they did along the border. They already controlled so much of the Arctic, the largest portion of any nation. In it were billions of dollars worth of oil and minerals, fish and water. What did they want with Norway beyond dominance, and what could Norway really do but submit?

WHEN I VISITED THE *OBSERVER* FOR THE LAST TIME, I brought cake. The bakery in downtown Kirkenes offered chocolate or strawberry, and I asked the woman at the counter which I should buy.

"Is this for Norwegians or Russians?" she said.

"Both."

"Get chocolate, then. Russians like that, and Norwegians won't really care."

At the office, I sat with Nilsen in the break room. The portrait of Gorbachev was still sitting there, below the window. The paper had just moved to this office, in the former headquarters of a mining company, and Nilsen said he hadn't yet had time to get Gorbachev properly framed and mounted.

I asked Nilsen if he was hopeful about border relations and he said, "Yes, you must always be hopeful."

At the same time, he'd been using the word *evil* more often than at any other time in his life. That day he'd been following a story on Russian warplanes based in the Arctic that flew south in the night to launch missiles into Ukraine.

"Evil," he said.

For his part, Chentemirov was preparing a story about his own battle with the Russian justice system. A few months earlier, without warning, his name had appeared on the government's list of so-called "foreign agents." This was "the list" he'd referred to when we first met. Being listed was the government's way of announcing to the public that you were a traitor, though it stopped short of using that word. If you stayed in Russia after being listed, your life balanced on a knife's edge. You, your social media, your finances, all might be surveilled or hacked. You weren't allowed to take certain jobs or participate in politics. Anything irregular might get you locked up.

Over cake, Chentemirov told me the state had never really said why he'd been listed, beyond a vague claim that he had "opposed the special military operation in Ukraine." He planned to challenge his status in absentia in a Russian court, but he didn't think the case would go anywhere. Neither did his lawyer.

"But I can't just let the bastards win," he said.

I liked this about Chentemirov. And I knew the choice to leave Russia still weighed on him. Together he and his wife, a doctor, had made the decision quickly and well before he'd been listed. It was September 2022. The shadows had been growing longer; there were signs Chentemirov was being watched. He learned he'd been offered a job at the *Observer* and the couple decided right then to leave. Soon they'd packed their two kids into the car and were headed east, toward Finland, which was the closest open border.

There was a sense of urgency as they rolled up to the

line. Chentemirov and his wife had told their son what they planned to do, but they hadn't explained it to their daughter. They worried she might act strangely or do something to give it away. After they'd made it over, they told her. She'd burst into tears and screamed, *I hate you.*

After the cake was gone, I walked home with Chentemirov in the warm spring sunshine. Maybe it was late, maybe early. The sun was ceaseless and we weren't paying attention. Chentemirov had other things on his mind. The test for his driver's license. The prospect of a lifetime in Norway. I suddenly remembered an old question: What happens to a caribou people who lose their caribou? Maybe the same thing that happened to a Russian who couldn't go home. Each day the border was pushing, pressing Chentemirov to choose. He believed he still had a little time.

AT THE END OF ANY STORY, I THINK OF THE BEGINning. The questions I didn't ask, the places I didn't see. Fates of the people and animals I'd encountered. The suddenness of the border was a trigger for such wondering. I thought of the Fosheim wolves, who by then were probably all dead of old age or unlucky injury. Several Indigenous elders I had known, the last of the nomads, had passed, too. Jacob Atqittuq and Mark Morry, Clyde's father, along with Raymond Paneak, the elder who'd showed a classroom of Nunamiut kids how to butcher caribou. I could not find any more recent count of the Bathurst herd in the land of the Tłı̨chǫ, though I knew the Western Arctic, Clyde's herd, was still shrinking.

At all of these thresholds, I'd been able to see into the past and the future, and even along the Norwegian border this was true. What surprised me most here was how civilized everything appeared at the surface, while below it was riven with conflict. I am not speaking only of the invasion of Ukraine; that was just one manifestation. I am also thinking of the Nazi occupation and refugees flooding the border on bicycles. I am thinking of jammed aircraft GPS systems and bombers that fly out of the Arctic darkness to kill civilians a world away. I am thinking about how bent steel girders and shattered concrete had come to feel like an invasive species, some kind of infestation that crept up from the south.

This was the most violent Arctic I had seen, busy with real and imagined bloodshed. This Arctic stood far apart from the others. I wondered how it looked from the Russian side. If you traveled east, as I'd wanted to do long ago, over Siberia to the Chukchi Sea and up to the border of America, would it look the same? Would you sense violence there in the distance, over the sea along the final frontier?

ONE LATE AFTERNOON, I DROVE EAST TOWARD RUS-sia with a couple of young soldiers named Bjugg and Grimstad. We were going to a place they called "the German bridge," which crossed a small river, the Jakobselv, that formed the border. The Nazis had built it, then they'd rolled over it during their invasion of Arctic Russia. For some reason it was still mostly intact. An old road wound through the hills to reach the bridge, then continued on the other side. Four steel girders still spanned the water.

We got out of our military truck and walked up. The sky was bruised with rain clouds, the birches were thick with birdsong, mosquitoes everywhere. Grimstad looked at the girders and declared that the bridge was in good shape. All you needed to do was throw a few planks down and drive over. He'd heard the Russians kept some stashed in the woods, just in case.

Then the young soldiers told me a story, not well known in the West, of a time the Soviet army nearly stormed into Europe over this bridge. It was June 1968, halfway through a year so tumultuous it's often compared to our own chaotic era of plagues and wars, of political and social unraveling. One day early in the month, thousands of Soviet troops and tanks began amassing along the border right above the German bridge. The weather was bad, so at first the soldiers stationed nearby only heard it—a great thrum of engines. Then the skies cleared and they saw an invasion force aimed right at them.

The conscripts called their superiors, who told them to fill their pockets with ammunition and take up their positions. You can almost imagine the looks on the men's faces. There were only a few dozen of them along the entire border, facing an army of thousands. But they were obedient Norwegians, and so they hunkered down and waited for the world to end.

After two or three days, the Soviets pulled their troops back. It had all been for show, perhaps, though the reasons were unclear. The Norwegian government never said much about the incident. Not many people down south ever knew how close they'd come to war.

Bjugg and Grimstad and I thought about it quietly for a few minutes. They were the conscripts now, waiting for the end.

Bjugg said, "We're just speed bumps."

"Maybe just potholes," said Grimstad.

Maybe less than either.

We stood shoulder to shoulder in the great vibrating wilderness. We stared over the river into Russia, imagining apocalypses. It was easier to do that here, perhaps because of the way the Arctic earth held the entangled past so lightly and almost within reach—era upon era, line upon line. As though it were trying to give it all back.

I thought again of the wolves and how the soil of their tundra seemed made of bones. I thought of the fierce brevity of their lives, and how their world was so opposite to this one. I had come as far as I could.

Clouds of fat, slow mosquitoes were driving us back to the truck when a spectacular double rainbow broke through the clouds. We stopped in our tracks, grinning wide and forgetting the bugs. One of the rainbows vanished far above the trees, but the other descended over the road in front of us. I had never seen such color. It seemed so close, an invitation of light.

All you needed to do was walk over the water.

# ACKNOWLEDGMENTS

When I began this project I had no idea what it would require of me, and even less what it would ask of others. Now,
at the end, I stand in awe of the help that was offered to me
all along the way, even when I didn't think I needed it and
sometimes when I at first stubbornly or unknowingly refused it. First let me thank the Indigenous nations and tribes
and bands whose lands I traveled over and through in the
places that are now called Alaska, Canada, Greenland, and
Norway. A partial list of these includes the Netsilingmiut,
Utkuhiksalingmiut, Tununirusirmiut, and the Inuvialuit,
all of whom are often grouped together under the broader
term Inuit; the Nunamiut, who are part of the larger Iñupiat; the Tłı̨chǫ, who are sometimes called Dogrib; the
Kalaallit of Greenland (who are also Inuit); and the Sami
people of Norway. For generations all of these people have
been generously sharing their stories and experiences with
outsiders, usually without any control or input over what
happens to it all. It must be noted that these people have
shared in the face of incredible settler violence, and even
as their own communities face unanswered hardships
that can almost always be traced to root causes down
south. This book simply would not have been possible
without the expansive generosity and patience of northern
people, and I am humbly grateful.

Together with those individuals who are named in the book, I also wish to thank Paul Ikuallaq, who took me hunting and admonished me to eat more, Vicky Monaghan, John B. Zoe, Josef Motzfeldt, Louisa Riley, and Cody Mantla, who gave me dried caribou meat. Several elders and others I spent time with have also died since this project began, and I think of them often. In memoriam, then: Mark Morry, Raymond Paneak, Jacob Atqittuq, and Ben Hopson III.

My debts are great to the many scientists and researchers I interviewed, spent time with, called on for guidance, or troubled with my endless questions. Without their curiosity and doggedness, and their willingness to share their discoveries and ideas, I would have skimmed surfaces only. In our time it isn't easy to be a scientist (has it ever been easy?), and it's even harder to open yourself and your work up to writers who will undoubtedly condense, summarize, and otherwise take shortcuts through long years of labor. Among those I wish to thank are the people who appear in earlier pages by name and the many more who don't, including Margaret B. Blackman, Robert Park, Peter Schledermann, Douglas Stenton, Greg Henry, Jette Arneborg, Kari Myklebost, Kira Cassidy, Greg Breed, Gita Ljubicic, Doug Stern, Grant Spearman, Mitch Campbell, Lincoln Parrett, Steve Ferguson, Elana and Lars Rowe, Peter Steen Henriksen, Dean Cluff, Alex Hansen, Karsten Heuer, Heather Johnson, Douglas Anderson, Elie Gurarie, Yun Sun, Jonathan Markowitz, Michael Byers, and Michael Sfraga.

In Kotzebue, Alaska, retired biologist Jim Dau and his wife, Randy Meyers, became my good friends, and even once flew up in their small plane to meet me on a lonely gravel bar on the North Slope where I had camped to look for caribou. Conversations with them were enlightening and led me toward questions I wouldn't have formed on my own. In Ambler, Don and Mary Williams were gracious hosts who also shared meat and seal oil and memories of how much the landscape had changed during their long lives. Seth Kantner, also in Kotzebue, was good company and is a wonderful writer.

During research for this book I stayed in many places and sometimes was helped along the road by a town, or a community, or even a school system. I want to specifically thank the North Slope Borough School District and the Nunamiut School in Anaktuvuk Pass, and the Northwest Arctic Borough School District and the Ambler School, along with their staffs, teachers, and principals. Employees of the town government in Anaktuvuk were also incredibly kind and patient.

In the Northwest Territories, I'm indebted to the Tłı̨chǫ Nation and the Tłı̨chǫ government, and to the staff of the Ekwǫ̀ Nàxoèhde K'è (Boots on the Ground) program, including Petter Jacobsen and Tyanna Steinwand. During the early phase of the Covid-19 pandemic I was also aided—or more accurately, tolerated—by officials of the territorial government. I also wish to thank the staff of the Eureka Weather Station on Ellesmere Island, in particular Jane Fonger, who answered so many of our questions and shared of her experiences in that inimitable place. The unstoppable Sarah McNair-Landry made it possible for us to work on Ellesmere.

One of the lasting frustrations in my work is the great mass of stories that don't make it into print. There are many untold ones gathered behind these pages, and for some of those I want to thank Norway's coast guard, the Kystvakt, and the sailors of the icebreaker KV *Svalbard*; as well as the soldiers of Garrison Sør-Varanger, particularly the Jarfjiord Company. I am also indebted to the staff of the weather station on the island of Bjørnøya, and to the staff of *The Barents Observer*, in Kirkenes, who abided my questions and loitering even as they tried to file their stories.

Nearer to home I am grateful to colleagues at Market Road Films, including Laura Colleluori, and to Tony Gerber and Lynn Nottage, whose creative generosity and collaboration not only helped me get back to the Arctic but also guided me in finding space to write later. I am sincerely grateful for time at Yaddo and my cohort there, who tolerated wolf stories and inspired me with their own incredible work. Thanks to Factual, and Wudan Yan, Mashal Butt, and Rachel Fobar for fact-checking on this project.

Many of these chapters began, or were in some way conceived, during my work over many years for *National Geographic*. I owe much to two editors in particular: Lisa Moore, who first took a chance on me, gave me a job, and sent me to the Arctic; and Karen Kostyal, who did the same sort of thing a little later on. I'm grateful for many years of collaboration at the magazine with a host of other editors, designers, and fact-checkers, and also for a small group of photographers with whom I traveled in the north. These folks are a special breed, and with them I had many wonderful adventures, some serious misadventures, days of fascinating conversations, and even heated (but ultimately helpful) arguments. They include Paul Nicklen, with whom I first worked in the Arctic, Louie Palu, Ronan Donovan, and Katie Orlinsky, who generously contributed photographs to this book. All of them taught me to see in new ways. I am also thankful to a pair of photographers I did not get to travel north with but who nevertheless offered thoughts and encouragement (as well as beautiful images) on the Russian Arctic, which I still hope to visit: they are Evgenia Arbugaeva and Yuri Kozyrev. My longtime editor at *National Geographic*, Peter Gwin, is a close friend, an excellent reader and writer, and in many ways an enabler of this book. I owe him much for his steadfastness and encouragement, and I'm glad I was able to wrest him free from the office to join me in Alaska.

There is no way I can sufficiently thank my editor at Ecco, Sarah Murphy, for all of her effort. She has been one of the most supportive and thoughtful people I've ever worked with, and her patience with me has been unlimited. The book, if it is good, is so because she guided it there. Thank you, Sarah. I also owe thanks to the team at Ecco, including Frieda Duggan, who saved me from my own messes. Profound gratitude goes to my agent, Susan Canavan, who both found me and understood the special sort of prodding I needed to do this thing.

To Luke Padgett and Adam Amir, companions on the land and in the mind, I return again and again. Thank you for reading and for joining me through all these places, in one way or another. Luke, thank you for making the map with me and editing photos.

Finally I want to thank my family. Without the help and encouragement, material support, and childcare of family, I would not have been able to finish this book. They include Emily, Rob, and Colin Hom; Andrew, Doug, and Jon Shea; and my own parents, Thomas and Jane, to whom I am forever grateful.

# SELECTED BIBLIOGRAPHY

Amundsen, Roald. *Roald Amundsen's Diaries from the Northwest Passage 1900–1907*. The Fram Museum, 2018.

Arneborg, Jette. "Change of Diet of the Greenland Vikings Determined from Stable Carbon Isotope Analysis and 14C Dating of Their Bones." *Radiocarbon*, January 1, 1999.

——. "Norse Greenland Dietary Economy ca. AD 980–ca. AD 1450: Introduction." *Journal of the North Atlantic Special* 3 (2012): 1–39.

Bessason, Haraldur, and Robert J. Glendenning, eds. *The Book of Settlements: Landnámabók*. Translated by Hermann Pálsson and Paul Edwards. University of Manitoba Press, 2007.

Blackman, Margaret B. *Upside Down: Seasons Among the Nunamiut*. University of Nebraska Press, 2004.

Bown, Stephen R. *White Eskimo: Knud Rasmussen's Fearless Journey into the Heart of the Arctic*. Douglas & McIntyre, 2015.

Brandenburg, Jim, and James S. Thornton. *White Wolf: Living with an Arctic Legend*. NorthWord Press, 1988.

Briggs, Jean L. *Never in Anger: Portrait of an Eskimo Family*. Harvard University Press, 1971.

Brown, Adrienne M. *Emergent Strategy: Shaping Change, Changing Worlds*. AK Press, 2017.

Buckland, Paul C., Thomas Amorosi, L. K. Barlow, et al. "Bioarchaeological and Climatological Evidence for the Fate of Norse Farmers in Medieval Greenland." *Antiquity* 70, no. 267 (March 1996).

Burch, Ernest S., Jr. *Caribou Herds of Northwest Alaska, 1850–2000*. University of Alaska Press, 2012.

Chester, Sharon R. *The Arctic Guide: Wildlife of the Far North*. Princeton University Press, 2016.

Demuth, Bathsheba. *Floating Coast: An Environmental History of the Bering Strait*. W. W. Norton & Company, 2020.

Dick, Lyle. *Muskox Land: Ellesmere Island in the Age of Contact*. University of Calgary Press, 2001.

Eber, Dorothy Harley. *Encounters on the Passage: Inuit Meet the Explorers*. University of Toronto Press, 2013.

Ehrlich, Gretel. *This Cold Heaven: Seven Seasons in Greenland*. Pantheon Books, 2001.

Gerin-Lajoie, Jose. *The Caribou Taste Different Now: Inuit Elders Observe Climate Change.* Nunavut Arctic College, 2016.

Gurarie, Eliezer, Mark Hebblewhite, Kyle Joly, et al. "Tactical Departures and Strategic Arrivals: Divergent Effects of Climate and Weather on Caribou Spring Migrations." *Ecosphere* 10 (December 12, 2019).

Hall, Edwin S. *The Eskimo Storyteller: Folktales from Noatak, Alaska.* University of Alaska Press, 1998.

Hayes, Derek. *Historical Atlas of the Arctic.* Douglas & McIntyre, 2003.

Heuer, Karsten. *Being Caribou: Five Months on Foot with an Arctic Herd.* McClelland & Stewart, 2007.

Holtsmark, Anne, and Jarle Rosseland, eds. *The Vinland Saga.* J. Rosseland, 2000.

Ingold, Tim. *Correspondences.* Polity, 2021.

Ingold, Tim, ed. *What Is an Animal?* Routledge, 1994.

Ingstad, Helge. *Nunamiut: Among Alaska's Inland Eskimos.* Allen & Unwin, 1954.

Ingstad, Helge, ed. *Nunamiut Unipkaanich / Nunamiut Stories.* Translated by Knut Bergsland. North Slope Borough Commission on Iñupiat History, Language and Culture, 1987.

Jackson, Rowan. "Archaeological Sites as Distributed Long-Term Observing Networks of the Past (DONOP)." *Quaternary International*, n.d.

Jackson, Rowan, Jette Arneborg, Andrew Dugmore, et al. "Success and Failure in the Norse North Atlantic: Origins, Pathway Divergence, Extinction and Survival." In *Perspectives on Public Policy in Societal-Environmental Crises: What the Future Needs from History.* Edited by Adam Izdebski, John Haldon, and Piotr Filipkowski. Springer 2022.

Jackson, Rowan, Jette Arneborg, and Thomas McGovern. "Disequilibrium, Adaptation, and the Norse Settlement of Greenland." *Human Ecology*, January 1, 2018.

Jackson, Rowan, Steven Hartman, Benjamin Trump, et al. "Disjunctures of Practice and the Problems of Collapse." In *Perspectives on Public Policy in Societal-Environmental Crises: What the Future Needs from History.* Edited by Adam Izdebski, John Haldon, and Piotr Filipkowski. Springer, 2022.

Joly, Kyle, Eliezer Gurarie, Mathew S. Sorum, et al. "Longest Terrestrial Migrations and Movements Around the World." *Scientific Reports* 9, no. 1 (October 25, 2019): 15333.

Kantner, Seth. *A Thousand Trails Home: Living with Caribou.* Mountaineers Books, 2021.

Kavenna, Joanna. *The Ice Museum: In Search of the Lost Land of Thule.* Viking Penguin, 2006.

Kimmerer, Robin Wall. *Braiding Sweetgrass: Indigenous Wisdom, Scientific Knowledge, and the Teachings of Plants.* Milkweed Editions, 2013.

*Kingdom of the White Wolf.* Documentary. Market Road Films, 2019.

Laffoon, Jason. "Jette Arneborg, Jan Heinemeier, and Niels Lynnerup. Greenland Isotope Project: Diet in Norse Greenland AD 1000–AD 1450 (JONA Special Volume 3). 2012. Steuben (ME): *Journal of the North Atlantic;* ISSN 1935–1984 Ebook." *Antiquity* 87, no. 337 (September 1, 2013): 932–34.

Laugrand, Frédéric B., and Jarich Gerlof Oosten. *Hunters, Predators and Prey: Inuit Perceptions of Animals.* Berghahn Books, 2014.

Legat, Allice. *Walking the Land, Feeding the Fire: Knowledge and Stewardship Among the Tłįchǫ Dene.* University of Arizona Press, 2012.

Lent, Peter C. *Muskoxen and Their Hunters: A History.* University of Oklahoma Press, 1999.

Lopez, Barry. *Arctic Dreams.* Simon and Schuster, 2024.

———. *Of Wolves and Men.* Simon and Schuster, 2024.

Lysenko, Dmitry, and Stephan Schott. "Food Security and Wildlife Management in Nunavut." *Ecological Economics* 156 (February 1, 2019): 360–74, https://doi.org/10.1016/j.ecolecon.2018.10.008.

Madsen, Christian Koch. "Pastoral Settlement, Farming, and Hierarchy in Norse Vatnahverfi, South Greenland." Unpublished PhD thesis. University of Copenhagen, n.d.

Malaurie, Jean. *The Last Kings of Thule: With the Polar Eskimos, as They Face Their Destiny.* Dutton, 1982.

Marquard-Petersen, Ulf. "Invasion of Eastern Greenland by the High Arctic Wolf *Canis Lupus Arctos.*" *Wildlife Biology* 17, no. 4 (December 2011): 383–88.

McGovern, Thomas H. "Cows, Harp Seals, and Churchbells: Adaptation and Extinction in Norse Greenland." *Human Ecology* 8, no. 3 (1980): 245.

Mech, L. David. "Alpha Status, Dominance, and Division of Labor in Wolf Packs." *Canadian Journal of Zoology* 77, no. 8 (November 1, 1999): 1196–1203, https://doi.org/10.1139/z99-099.

———. *The Arctic Wolf: Living with the Pack.* Voyageur Press, 1988.

———. *The Arctic Wolf: Ten Years with the Pack.* Swan Hill, 1997.

———. "Possible Use of Foresight, Understanding, and Planning by Wolves Hunting Muskoxen." *ARCTIC* 60, no. 2 (December 11, 2009): 145–49.

Meyer, Connor J., Kira A. Cassidy, Erin E. Stahler, et al. "Parasitic Infection Increases Risk-Taking in a Social, Intermediate Host Carnivore." *Communications Biology* 5, no. 1 (2022): 1180.

Nansen, Fridtjof. *Farthest North: Being the Record of a Voyage of Exploration of the Ship Fram, 1893–96, and of a Fifteen Months' Sleigh Journey by Dr. Nansen and Lieut. Johansen.* Harper & Brothers, 1897.

Panagiotakopulu, Eva, M. T. Greenwood, and Paul Buckland. "Irrigation and Manuring in Medieval Greenland." *Geografiska Annaler Series A Physical Geography* 94, no. 4 (January 2012): 531–48.

Paneak, Simon, and John Martin Campbell. *In a Hungry Country*. University of Alaska Press, 2004.

Pedersen, Dorthe Dangvard, and Jette Arneborg. "Excavations at the Churchyard in Igaliku, the Norse Bishop See at Gardar, July 2019: KNK 4201," January 15, 2020.

Post, Eric. *Time in Ecology: A Theoretical Framework*. Princeton University Press, 2019.

Price, Neil. *Children of Ash and Elm: A History of the Vikings*. Basic Books, 2022.

Rasmussen, Knud. *Across Arctic America: Narrative of the Fifth Thule Expedition*. G. P. Putnam's Sons, 1927.

———. *Eskimo Poems from Canada and Greenland*. Translated by Tom Lowenstein. University of Pittsburgh Press, 1973.

Rausch, Robert. "Notes on the Nunamiut Eskimo and Mammals of the Anaktuvuk Pass Region, Brooks Range, Alaska." *ARCTIC* 4, no. 3 (January 1, 1951): 146–95.

Rowe, Lars. *Pollution and Atmosphere in Post-Soviet Russia: The Arctic and the Environment*. Bloomsbury Academic, 2021.

Safina, Carl. *Beyond Words: What Animals Think and Feel*. Henry Holt and Company, 2015.

Schledermann, Peter. *Voices in Stone: A Personal Journey into the Arctic Past*. Arctic Institute of North America of the University of Calgary, 1996.

Schleidt, Wolfgang M., and Michael D. Shalter. "Dogs and Mankind: Coevolution on the Move—An Update." *Human Ethology Bulletin* 33, no. 1 (March 25, 2018): 15–38.

Steeves, Paulette F. C. *The Indigenous Paleolithic of the Western Hemisphere*. University of Nebraska Press, 2021.

Walker, Brett L. *Lost Wolves of Japan*. University of Washington Press, 2009.

Watt-Cloutier, Sheila. *The Right to Be Cold: One Woman's Story of Protecting Her Culture, the Arctic and the Whole Planet*. Penguin Random House Canada, 2016.

Wilson, Ryan R., Lincoln S. Parrett, Kyle Joly, and Jim R. Dau. "Effects of Roads on Individual Caribou Movements During Migration." *Biological Conservation* 195 (March 1, 2016): 2–8, https://doi.org/10.1016/j.biocon.2015.12.035.

# INDEX